THE
SIGNIFICANCE
OF THE
CHURCH

THE LAYMAN'S THEOLOGICAL LIBRARY
Robert McAfee Brown, *General Editor*

The
Significance
of the
Church

by
Robert McAfee Brown

LAYMAN'S
THEOLOGICAL
LIBRARY

THE WESTMINSTER PRESS

PHILADELPHIA

Acknowledgment is made for permission to quote from the following:

" The Rock " and " The Hippopotamus " in *Collected Poems of T. S. Eliot*. Harcourt, Brace and Company, Inc.

" Meditation for a Young Boy Confirmed," by Alan Paton. *The Christian Century,* October 13, 1954, p. 1239.

Library of Congress Catalog Card No.: 56–6172

PRINTED IN THE UNITED STATES OF AMERICA

281
c. 2

Contents

5

FOREWORD

The religious book market is full of books for "the intelligent layman." Some are an insult to his intelligence. Others are covertly written for professional theologians. A few are genuine helps in communicating the faith.

In this spate of books being thrust at the lay reader, what distinctive place can the Layman's Theological Library claim to hold? For one thing, it will try to remind the layman that he *is* a theologian. The close conjunction of the words "layman" and "theological" in the title of the series is not by chance but by design. For theology is not an irrelevant pastime of seminary professors. It is the occupation of every Christian, the moment he begins to think about, or talk about, or communicate, his Christian faith. The injunction to love God *with all his mind,* necessarily involves the layman in theology. He can never avoid theology; if he refuses to think through his faith, he simply settles for an inferior theology.

Furthermore, the Layman's Theological Library will attempt to give a *wholeness* in its presentation of the Christian faith. Its twelve volumes cover the main areas of Christian faith and practice. They are written out of similar convictions which the authors share about the uniqueness of the Christian faith. All the authors are convinced that Christian faith can be made relevant, that it can be made understandable without becoming innocuous, and that (particularly in view of the current "return to religion") it is crucially important for the layman

7

to commit himself to more than "religion in general." The Layman's Theological Library, then, will attempt a fresh exploration of the Christian faith, and what it can mean in the life of twentieth-century man.

There is nothing in this particular book that cannot be found in a dozen other books. But because laymen probably don't have time to read a dozen books about the Church, this one attempts to pull together for them some of the things that Christians, standing broadly in the Protestant Reformed tradition, have believed about the Church.

Some people will say, "Why isn't there a chapter on the ecumenical movement?" or, "Why isn't he tougher on the Roman Catholics?" I can only acknowledge that somebody else might have done it quite differently, and that I have placed the emphases where they seemed important to me. I will be satisfied if this book gets people thinking about the Church in Reformation terms, and more than satisfied if through it they may even be led by God to a greater sense of dedication to the Church, and to Jesus Christ who is the head of the Church, and whom the Church exists to serve.

ROBERT MCAFEE BROWN

CHAPTER 1

A Long Hard Look at the Church

"Though with a scornful wonder
Men see her sore oppressed,
By schisms rent asunder,
By heresies distressed,
Yet saints their watch are keeping,
Their cry goes up, 'How long?'
And soon the night of weeping
Shall be the morn of song."

—*Stanza 3 of "The Church's One Foundation," almost invariably omitted from modern hymnals*

Many people who don't like hymns would offer a hearty "Amen!" to the first four lines printed above. These people *do* look at the Church with a "scornful wonder," and they see a Church in hot water ("sore oppressed"), split up into factions ("by schisms rent asunder"), and containing all sorts of people proclaiming all sorts of things, none of which seem to be true ("by heresies distressed").

"What an accurate description!" these people say. "Too bad the Church isn't willing to acknowledge the fact."

But there are four more lines. The language sounds a bit

9

out of date, to be sure (the words were written in 1866), but the point is clear: those within the Church express themselves as aware of the shocking state of things, and determined that it shall change.

Yet the stanza isn't sung any more. It may be that modern Christians aren't up to facing (*a*) the truth of the first four lines, or (*b*) the challenge of the last four lines. If that is so, then the Church can cheerfully be buried. But there may be persons both within and without the Church who *are* willing to do both of these things.

And it is to such people that this book is addressed.

The case against the Church — by the outsider:

> "The power of hell is strongest where
> The odor of sanctity fills the air."
> — *Saint Hereticus*

If we are really going to engage in a "long hard look at the Church," we must have the honesty to admit that there are a lot of things wrong with it. We must listen to the people who are willing to tell us so. Here they are, nine strong:

A Social Worker: I spend my week trying to change society. And do you know who furnishes the biggest obstacle to my work? The churches, and the "good solid church people." Ever try to get a church board interested in a slum-clearance project? I did, last week. I found that half of the members owned property in the slum, and would have no part of any project that might lower the income they were getting from it.

A Person with Humane Interests: The main thing the churches in our town do is to fight one another. There's a constant feud between the Protestants and Catholics. The Episcopalians and Baptists claim to worship the same God, but try to get them together for a Communion service! There's no fight quite so vicious as a church fight, whether it's over the new organist, or the color of the rug in the Ladies' Aid room.

A Person of Integrity: I want to be honest. And I simply can't be in church. Christians get up Sunday after Sunday with straight "religious" faces, and sing, "We are not divided, all one body we." Not divided? They're divided into so many fragments you can hardly count them. They repeat pious phrases about being "one in Christ Jesus," and at the very moment they are saying these things — 11 o'clock Sunday morning — America is at its segregated worst.

Another Person of Integrity: There's no group easier to join than a prosperous American church. You get in and then discover that you're one of the "2,000 members before Easter" they were out to snag, and that you're just helping to make the "third biggest Church" in the state.

A Person with "Good Taste": I once heard a minister use the phrase, "Worship the Lord in the beauty of holiness." He said it in the ugliest building I've ever been in. The hymns were a musical outrage. The preacher was incomprehensible. And did I mention the backs of those pews? . . .

A Person Disturbed About the State of the World: What do I hear in church? Either a lot of irrelevant nonsense about loving our enemies, or else a lot more nonsense about pearly gates, or a last judgment. I'm concerned about the next ten years. Will we blow ourselves to pieces before then? Are we going to have a war? Why doesn't the Church *do* something about these things?

An "Enlightened" Person: I believe in the Golden Rule and the Ten Commandments, but religion is an individual matter. What this world needs is more individuals who will live up to their ideals. We don't need churches for that. I believe in Christianity, but not Churchianity.

An Intellectual: I'm willing to bet that not ten per cent of the people who recite creeds, sing hymns, and read the Bible have the foggiest notion what's going on. " He descended into hell . . . He ascended into heaven." What kind of mumbo jumbo is this? "God in Three Persons, blessed Trinity! " What kind of mathematics is that? And the Bible! I simply can't believe in " the credibility of Genesis and the edibility of Jonah." I've read too much science.

An Outsider Who Would Like to Believe: I even belonged to a church for a while. And what happened? I was drafted for the men's bowling team, my wife was put on the kitchen crew for church supper after church supper (meat loaf every time), and when I put my son in the high school group, all they did was paint the kindergarten furniture or pop corn. I'm a comfortable pagan once more.

The case against the Church — by the insider:

" The Church is both holy and sinful. This is the fundamental root of the whole problem of the Church, that it is a union of sinful souls with the Holy God." — *Lesslie Newbigin, Bishop of the Church of South India.*

The outsiders have offered a formidable indictment. But the surprising thing is that the insider — if he is honest — can often give a more damning indictment of the Church than anyone else. In fact, by this time he is ready with quite a little speech:

"Certainly these things are true. I could document each charge more vividly than any of the outsiders have done. Let's consider their case proved. I only wish that were *all* that had to be said! But I'm afraid there's still more.

"Two kinds of things particularly upset me: Churches setting themselves up as the *only* gateway to heaven, and, at the other extreme, Churches that are so 'open' and 'liberal' that they really don't stand for anything. This is what worries me about the current 'return to religion.' People are filling the churches — but I'm not sure they are getting more than soothing spiritual pats on the back. The 'peace' is too easy. The 'religion' makes no demands. It doesn't bear much resemblance to the New Testament.

"And this brings to mind the really surprising omission in the outsiders' indictment. They missed one of the best reasons why people get fed up with the Church. T. S. Eliot describes this better than I can in his poem "The Rock":

"'Why should men love the Church? Why should they love her laws?
She tells them of Life and Death, and of all that they would forget.
She is tender where they would be hard, and hard where they like to be soft.
She tells them of Evil and Sin, and other unpleasant facts.'

"I'm not saying the Church should always talk about 'unpleasant facts.' That's not the good news, after all. But I am saying that authentic Christianity doesn't make people feel better just as they are. It talks about starting again, being changed, and a number of other inconvenient things, all of which demand admitting that you're not so great the way you are.

There's a *real* reason for people to be offended by the Church — because its message is bound to offend as well as to heal.

"This means that when I look at the shortcomings of the Church, I can't charge them up to somebody else. I can't say, 'It's *their* fault'; I have to say (and it's no fun), 'It's *my* fault.' Because, most of the time, I would rather be on the men's bowling team than working on a slum-clearance project; I would rather have 'the Church stay out of politics' than have to vote on the basis of Christian conscience.

"I can't help noticing that the outsider almost always judges what the Church *is* by what the Church *ought to be*. It would be great, he thinks, to have an all-embracing fellowship, or a society concerned about injustice. I couldn't agree more.

"But here's the difference. The outsider says, in effect, 'I won't touch the Church until it reforms,' whereas the insider tries to say (and I hope it doesn't sound too priggish), 'I've got to be involved in the reform myself.' It's a little bit like political democracy. It would be a sorry thing for democracy if people refused to vote while there were still hypocrites in politics, corrupt party machines, and ward rallies held in dingy surroundings. Fortunately (for democracy) people don't apply the same logic there that they apply to the Church. They acknowledge that it is more significant to be an 'insider' than an 'outsider.' They work within the system to improve the system.

"Without pressing the similarities too far (God isn't a party 'boss' who's up for re-election) it seems to me that the same kind of logic applies to the Church.

"And another thing. The outsider's picture isn't the whole picture. A lot of evidence has been omitted. It's like this . . ."

Here we must interrupt the insider. For he is starting to steal a few leaves from the later pages of this book.

The other side of the outsider's picture:

"I AM SCERCHING FOR A NEW HOUSE FOR OWL SO HAD YOU RABBIT."

— *The Mysterious Missage left under Winnie-the-Pooh's front door*

We haven't finished looking at the world of the outsider. He isn't too happy about the Church. But he isn't too happy about the rest of the world, either. He acknowledges, in language that is almost literally true, that it's a hell of a world. What is the trouble?

We shall not take a lot of time " analyzing the world situation " so that we can come up, ten pages hence, with the triumphant (and empty) assertion that " the Church has all the answers." But let us look briefly at *one* characteristic of this twentieth-century world, which may provide us with a clue as to the plight of the outsider.

That characteristic is *the desire for community*. Or, put the other way around, it is *the dislike of isolation and aloneness*. People want to *belong*. It is too frightening to be alone — or too boring. And rather than remain in total isolation, people join or create communities. If the old ones (like the Church) seem unsatisfactory, then we find them, like Rabbit, " scerching for a new house." And there are plenty.

1. The most potent expression of community in the last hundred years has been the Communist cell. For millions of Asians, if not Americans, Communism is the greatest redemptive hope alive today. If you are a Communist, you are part of the group. You are no longer alone. You are dedicated to a great cause. You share a goal (and sometimes a secret) with other people. You *belong*.

2. There are hundreds of other groups that try to satisfy this desire for community: Elks, Moose, Masons, Rotary, Kiwanis, Knights of Columbus, Red Men, Daughters of the American Revolution, the American Legion. Even Penrod and his friends had their " Innapenent Order of Infadelaty."

3. Another attempt to provide community is the cocktail party. Someone has said that the cocktail party is a secularized version of the Lord's Supper. The suggestion may shock, which it probably was intended to do, but it is worth following up. It is an outward and visible sign (getting together) of an inward invisible grace (the feeling that "we belong together"). There are the elements (wafers — or *hors d'oeuvres* — and wine). There is a priest (the host) or a priestess (the hostess) who dispenses the elements. The communion is usually "closed communion" (only certain people are admitted). There is, in short, a frantic effort to achieve communal feeling; frantic, since the communicants cannot achieve it on their own, and must be helped by repeated trips to the source of new life (the bottle) " from which all blessings flow."

The point is simply this: In a world where people feel so lost and alone that they eagerly (and sometimes pathetically) desire community, it makes sense once more to talk about the *Christian* community. Let us not claim too much for the argument. It does not mean that a recognition of this fact will send people flocking to the churches. It does not mean that even if they did come, the churches would know what to do with them. It does not mean that the Church is a community in the same sense that Communists, Kiwanis, and cocktails are signs of community. But at least it means that talk about community is not irrelevant. And the existence of a particular community — the Church — may be more significant than we have realized.

The other side of the insider's picture:

" The Church is something like Noah's ark. If it weren't for the storm outside, you couldn't stand the smell inside." — *A late medieval manuscript.*

" This Catholic Church hath been sometimes more, sometimes less, visible." — *The Westminster Confession of Faith* (*1648*).

We must give the insider one more word. Why are there Christians who " love the Church " (in Eliot's phrase) and identify themselves with it?

1. It is clear that from the very first Christian faith *was* community rather than just the faith of scattered individuals. For example, in almost every place that the phrase " in Christ " occurs in Paul's letters, it means " in the Christian community." It does not stand for a private kind of mysticism. To be " in Christ " is to be " in the Church." The term " individual Christianity " cancels itself out. Anyone who takes Christianity seriously is forced to take the Church seriously.

2. The Church is the means by which the Christian faith is " passed on." Without the Church, no Christians after a few generations. It is the Church that has kept men and nations and generations confronted with the demands and the prom ises of Christ. This is a matter of simple, historic fact.

3. The Church is a community in a very special sense. It is not just a voluntary fellowship of people who think it a " good idea " to get together occasionally. The authentic Christian note is that the Church is a community created by God, called into existence by him, and dependent upon him for its very life and energy. (We will examine this far-reaching claim in Chs.

3 and 4.) Christ is the Head of the Church, not some district superintendent, or bishop, or congregation.

4. Those who "love the Church" do so not only despite its limitations, but because the Church has power in their lives.

For the Church *has been* a community of grace, a place where men have come to know God's love, and been empowered by that love to love their fellow men.

The Church *has been* a place where barriers of race and nation and color have been overcome. Many people have first discovered *in the Church* that "all are one in Christ Jesus," and that in him "there is no East or West."

The Church *has been* a place where men have discovered not only what it means to be forgiven, but also what it means to forgive. And where forgiveness is real, no limits can be placed upon the creative power which can be unleashed.

Alan Paton has put in a few lines something of what the Church means to the believer. After describing the way God "laid His yoke upon me, and bound me with these chains, that I have worn with no especial grace," he continues:

"Why then I did accept this miracle, and being what I am
    some lesser miracles,
And then I did accept this Faith, and being what I am
    some certain Articles,
And then I did accept this Law, and being what I am some
    regulations,
Why then I worshiped Him, and being what I am knelt in
    some pew
And heard some organ play and some bells peal, and heard
    some people sing,
And heard about some money that was wanted, and heard
    some sin was preached against,

And heard some message given by some man, sometimes
   with great distinction, sometimes none.
I made this humble access, I too stretched out my hands,
Sometimes I saw Him not, and sometimes clearly, though
   with my inward eyes.
I stayed there on my knees, I saw His feet approaching,
I saw the mark of the nails, I did not dare to look fully
   at them.
I longed to behold Him, I did not dare to behold Him,
I said in my heart to Him, I who in sins and doubts and
   in my grievous separation reach out my hands,
Reach out Thy hands and touch me, oh most Holy One."

1517 — AND ALL THAT,
. . . With an Exercise in Vocabulary

"But what are these new doctrines? The gospel? Why,
that is 1,522 years old. The teaching of the apostles?
Why, they are almost as old as the gospel. . . . We will
try everything by the touchstone of the gospel and the
fire of Paul." — *Philip Melanchthon, one of the Protestant Reformers, in 1522.*

To most people, October 31 means only one thing — Hal-
loween, with its black cats, ghosts, and goblins. But increasing
numbers of Protestants are learning that the Sunday nearest
October 31, called Reformation Sunday, is a time when there
is special reason to remember a particular October 31 — the
one in 1517, to be exact.

Why look to the past? If you want to know something
about Julius Caesar or Davy Crockett, you read a biography,
to learn what influences worked on them, what the decisive
events in their lives were, and so on. The same thing is true
about the Church. You can't start "cold" with the twentieth
century. You need to know how the Church got started, what
the decisive events in its history were, how it "got the way it
is today."

And so in this chapter we shall look at the most decisive event in the life of the Church, the Protestant Reformation of the sixteenth century. This is not the "beginning" of the Church. We will look at that in the next chapter. But it is the point in the Church's history from which we can best understand both its beginnings and the state of its present life.

The Reformation as the recovery of the gospel:

"Eŭangelīo (that we cal gospel) is a greke word, and signifyth good, mery, glad and joyful tydings, that maketh a mannes hert glad, and maketh hym synge, daunce and leepe for ioye." — *William Tyndale, a "pre-reformer" who was burned at the stake for daring to translate the New Testament into English.*

"Why did a group of 'reformers' break away from the Church after fifteen hundred years and start a new religion?"

To ask the question this way is to miss the point from the very beginning. For if there is anything that the Reformers were *not* doing, it was inventing a new religion or a new Church. They were doing precisely the opposite.

Consider the Christian Church as a ship that had been sailing on the sea of history for a long time. It had picked up a great many barnacles, which made it hard to keep it on its proper course. It had been through such severe storms that some of its equipment had gotten washed overboard. What the Reformers did was to take the ship into dry dock, chip off the barnacles, and restore the lost equipment, so that *the same ship* could be launched again and fulfill its proper task.

This means that the Reformers didn't invent the gospel they proclaimed. They were trying to revive the "old" religion,

described in the New Testament, and make it once again
normative for Christendom. They were trying to re-establish
continuity with their authentic past. The assertions that they
wanted to inaugurate the "era of private judgment," or "split
the Church," or "replace God's truth with man-made truths,"
are spectacularly wide of the mark.

To be sure, the word "protestant" sounds negative: pro-
testing *against* the pope, or higher taxes, or injustice. But the
Latin *protestari* actually means to testify on behalf of something, to engage in positive testimony. Webster's dictionary
uses "affirm" as a synonym. The Reformers were affirming
their fidelity to the Christian faith. They were engaging in
positive testimony.

So the next question is obvious. What was the content of
their positive testimony? To what faith were they trying to
recall the Church?

What happened to Luther and what difference does it make?

On October 31, 1517, an Augustinian monk, one Martin
Luther, nailed Ninety-five Theses to the door of the castle
church at Wittenberg. There was nothing dramatic about it.
All he was doing was offering to debate the truth or falsity of
ninety-five short propositions or "theses" having to do with
beliefs of the medieval Church. Nobody even turned up to accept Luther's challenge. But this is the event about which people, looking back, can say: "There was the turning point.
After that, things were never really the same again." It is about
as close as we can come to "dating" the beginning of the
Reformation.

This was not the first time in Luther's life that he had decided that all was not well with the Church. It was not, in fact,
the first time in the Church's life that someone had decided

that all was not well. For, almost from its beginning, the Church has had reformers, men who felt that the Church was being faithless to its Lord and did not hesitate to say so. Saint Francis, in Italy, calling for a radical simplification in the life of the Church; John Wycliffe, in England, anticipating many of the teachings of Luther and Calvin about Scripture, and translating the Bible into English; John Hus, in Bohemia, striking a blow for the layman — these men make it clear that for a number of centuries " all was not well " with the Church. But for a variety of reasons, it was in Martin Luther that all these yearnings came alive.

Luther was not merely concerned about abuses in the life of the Church, though there were plenty. The clergy were ignorant and immoral, the popes were clever and immoral, the finances of the Church were a scandal — these things are common knowledge to anybody who dips into the history of the period. But something deeper was at stake.

Luther had been instructed by his medieval faith that if you wanted to be in right relationship with God, you had to *earn* the right to his love, by doing " good works." You were " justified," or set right with God (or in modern slang, you became " O.K. with God ") on the basis of what you did. If you were good enough, God would love you. In order to ensure the salvation of his soul, Luther did not only all that was expected, but a good deal more. Rather than remaining a layman, he became a monk. Rather than doing the minimum " works " a monk was supposed to do, he did extra ones. But the more he tried, the more convinced he became that he could never do enough to earn God's love.

No matter how hard he tried, he was sure he could have tried harder.

No matter how many sins he confessed, he was sure there

were still more he should have confessed.

No matter how many good works he performed, he was sure there were still more that could have been done.

The way of "justification by works" was a dead-end street for anybody with a sensitive conscience.

And this was the point at which God, in his goodness, showed Luther the way out of his dilemma. For as Luther studied his Bible, particularly the Psalms, Galatians, and Romans, he came to see that the Biblical understanding of God's relationship to men was something very different from all this. Paul had been in the same "box" as Luther. Paul had tried to live by the "law"—the Jewish law in this case; he too had tried to be "justified by works." And it hadn't worked for Paul either. What Paul found, and what Luther rediscovered by reading Paul, was that men were set right with God, *not on the basis of what they could do for God, but on the basis of what God had done for them.*

This was a shattering reversal of the situation. It meant that rather than waiting until Paul and Luther were "worthy" of his love, God had offered his love to them while they were still unworthy. This is what they saw to be the meaning of the coming of Jesus Christ into the world. Here was God's answer. Not an answer that said, "Be good, and then I will come to you in love," but an answer that said: "I *have* come to you in love already, and given myself to you. Can't you believe that this is so?"

Luther came to believe that it *was* so. For God, in Christ, had come to men, and taken upon *himself* the burden of their wrongdoing (this is what Luther saw happening in the murder of Christ at the hands of men). The situation was now totally different. So Luther was "justified" or set right with God not by his "works"; he was justified by his "faith." Faith was no longer assent to the doctrines of the medieval Church; faith was *trust,* trust that the promises of God were true, trust that in Christ, God had really offered his forgiveness to all men. No longer did he have to try to earn God's love; all he had to do was accept God's love.

This, Luther felt and Protestants have felt ever since, is the heart of the gospel — the story of a gracious God who reaches out to his erring children in their need, and restores the broken relationship in an act of suffering love. The Church exists to proclaim this and to make it real.

Now of course, if this were true, then a whole bagful of questions had to be asked about the Church: Why should one try to " earn " forgiveness when it was a free gift? Why should the Church claim to dispense grace (for a fee) when it had no jurisdiction over it? Why shouldn't all people be allowed to read the Bible, which contained this good news? Why should Christians acknowledge a man as head of the Church when the true Head of the Church was Jesus Christ?

Luther wrestled with these questions (and lots more) for a good many years. He tried to make the leaders of the medieval Church see that their message was not the Christian gospel. But to no avail. And so Luther, in faithfulness to God's Word, had to stand against men's words. He had to be faithful to the gospel even when a whole Church seemed to be faithless. Other men picked up the strain. They continued what he started. They have been doing so ever since. They are the people called " Protestants."

An exercise in vocabulary:

There are two ways in which Christian faith can be proclaimed relevantly. A believer can use vocabulary drawn from his own time, avoiding the " traditional " words, which " people no longer understand." Or he can start with the traditional words and try to explain them in terms people *can* understand.

For better or for worse, we shall lean toward the second method in what follows. Protestant laymen must make an effort to understand their heritage. If they really did, the problem of relevance would begin to take care of itself. We shall look at seven emphases of Reformation Christianity. They do not exhaust the content of Christian faith, but they are always central for Protestants.

" Justification by Faith "

" You are accepted. All you need to do is to accept the fact that you are accepted." — *Paul Tillich, a contemporary Reformer.*

We have seen what " justification by faith " meant to Luther. Can this still have meaning today? Let us see if an analogy will help.

You are afraid to face yourself, or other people. You dislike them, you feel that they dislike you; you want to be with them and yet you are afraid to be with them. You need help.

Under what conditions can a psychiatrist help you? First, you have to acknowledge that you cannot help yourself. This you do by placing yourself in his hands. Second, you have to be convinced that *he accepts you just as you are now*. You need not be " worthy." No conditions are laid down, no demands are made. You are accepted just as you are. Third, as you come to see that you are accepted, you can begin to accept yourself, " live with yourself " once again. And finally you can begin to accept other people. You are being restored to a situation of health (which is what the word " salvation " originally meant).

Now what brought this about? You were not " saved " by doing good works to impress the psychiatrist. Your " salvation "
was made possible by your faith in the psychiatrist's acceptance
of you "just as you were." And without making the assumption that God is a Great Big Psychiatrist, the analogy clarifies
the fact that in a relationship with God, the significant thing
is *God's acceptance,* which makes possible all kinds of human
acceptance. Men are "justified" by their faith that God is an
" accepting " God. Which changes everything.*

The Place of " Works "

" Good works do not make a man good, but a good
man does good works." — *Martin Luther, who learned
the hard way.*

Does all this mean that " works " don't matter, that you can
do as you please since God will forgive you anyhow?

Such a charge has often been brought against the doctrine of
justification by faith, but it is based on a misunderstanding.
Certainly good works are important, but not as a means of procuring God's love and grace. *Rather than procuring it, they
flow from it.* The response of the person who has been accepted by God, even though " unacceptable," must be one of
gratitude and thankfulness. Luther describes the result:

" Well now! my God has given to me, unworthy and lost
man, without any merit, absolutely for nothing and out of pure
mercy, through and in Christ, the full riches of all godliness

* The Reformers also said that salvation was *sola gratia,* by
grace alone. This meant that right relationship with God is not
achieved by works but solely by God's grace, i.e., his outgoing love
offered to us.

and blessedness, so that I henceforth need nothing more than to believe it is so. Well, then, for such a Father, who has so prodigally lavished upon me his blessings, I will in return freely, joyously and for nothing do what is well-pleasing to him, and also be a Christian towards my neighbor, as Christ has been to me. . . . For just as our neighbor suffers want and is in need of our superabundance, so have we suffered want before God and been in need of his grace. Therefore, as God through Christ has helped us for nothing, so ought we through the body and its works to do nothing but help our neighbor."

"The Priesthood of All Believers"

"You are a chosen race, a royal priesthood, a holy nation, God's own people, that you may declare the wonderful deeds of him who called you out of darkness into his marvelous light." — *I Peter 2:9.*

But so far this sounds highly individualistic. And many people argue that the Reformers minimized the Church, claiming that the individual is all that matters.

This is a misunderstanding. The Reformers believed in the Church with utmost seriousness. It was precisely because of the sad state *of the Church* that they got perturbed. Their purpose was to reform the life *of the Church* — not just individuals. It was medieval Catholicism that was "individualistic," with private devotions (such as developed in the stations of the cross and the rosary) taking the place of corporate Christian life. It was the glory of the Reformers that they restored the life of the congregation, the people of God assembled *together* in his name.

And so the phrase "the priesthood of all believers" is very important. It does *not* mean, "Every man is his own priest, so no church is necessary," but rather, "Every man is a priest to

every other man, so community (or a church) is necessary."
The priest, the one who mediates God to his fellow men, is not
just an occasional individual in "holy orders," he is every
Christian, for all Christians are in "holy orders." The whole
Christian life is one of community, and the Christian life
without the people of God is an impossible notion.

"The Authority of Scripture"

"The Lord has more truth yet to break forth out of his
holy Word." — *John Robinson to the Pilgrims, as they
set sail for America.*

To believe in the authority of the Bible does not mean accepting the Bible as a repository of "proof texts" — though to
second-generation Reformers and some contemporary Protestants it has been twisted in that direction. The point is that by
exposing themselves to the Bible, Protestants come to hear the
Word of God as a Word addressed to *them.* God *does* let
"more truth break forth out of his holy Word," so that the
Bible is a contemporary book rather than a book from the past.
It was his study of the Bible that showed Luther that the center of salvation must be shifted from man to God. It is in the
Bible that Christians feel the impact of Jesus Christ, for as
Luther said, "The Bible is the cradle in which Christ lies."
Small wonder that he translated it into German so the com-
mon people could read it.

Protestants, then, live with the "open Bible." They seek to
guide their lives by it, not using it legalistically, but letting it be
the means by which God's Word in Jesus Christ becomes a
living Word today.*

* There are many problems raised for Protestants in attempting
to use the Bible. A later volume in this series, by Professor Fred
Denbeaux, will deal with these.

"The Sovereignty of God"

"God alone is Lord of the conscience."
— *The Westminster Confession of Faith* (*1648*)

The first volume in this series, Cornelius Loew's *Modern Rivals to Christian Faith,* has treated the problem of idolatry, or the worship of false gods, showing how this involves a drastic departure from Reformation Christianity. To give one's allegiance to any but the one true God is to depart from Christian faithfulness. "Thou shalt have no other gods before me," the first (and most important) of the Ten Commandments, was taken with utmost seriousness by the Reformers.

There are few more important emphases today when other "gods" are clamoring for worship. To believe in the sovereignty of God means that the Protestant can never give his final allegiance to the *State*. The State is not sovereign. God is sovereign. Nor can final allegiance be given to a *Church,* since a Church is composed of human beings who err and whose judgments are always something less than divine truth. (Here is one of the basic points of contention between Protestantism and Roman Catholicism.) One can never say, "My country right or wrong, may she be right, but right or wrong, my country." Nor can one say, "My labor union, right or wrong," "My corporation, right or wrong," nor even, "My theology, right or wrong." It is only to God himself that the Protestant can commit his life with total and absolute devotion. As Reinhold Niebuhr has put it, "We must fight their falsehood with our truth, but we must also fight the falsehood *in* our truth."

"The Doctrine of the 'Calling'"

"There are few more dangerous words than 'spiritual.'" — *Sir George MacLeod in* We Shall Rebuild.

Why so? Because absorption in "spiritual" things can make us blind to "material" responsibilities, and be a denial of life *in the world* as significant in God's sight. During the medieval period a distinction arose between the "sacred" and the "secular," particularly in terms of vocation. The highest calling was to be a monk, withdrawn from the evil world of men (and women). "Ordinary" Christians might remain in the sinful world as butchers or bakers, but theirs was a second-rate kind of Christian life.

The Reformers cut through that distinction and asserted that one's calling could be fulfilled in any vocation, and not just in a "sacred" one. As Luther put it, the shoemaker can serve God at his bench as fully as the priest at the altar. Calvin pointed out that instead of retiring to the monastery to serve God, the Christian should see the whole world as God's monastery, and serve God right where he was in the midst of the life of men. "The sacredness of the secular" was reaffirmed. All life was invested with meaning and all work was invested with dignity. The Reformation gave "the common life" back to man; man in his turn was to give it back to God.

As then, so today. God calls men to live *in* his world, rather than to flee from it. This spirit leads to "Christian citizenship," to responsible political activity, to concern for the destitute, and all the rest of man's social obligations. It remains a permanent contribution of the Reformation to the ordering of man's total life under God.

"The Doctrine of the Word"

"In the beginning was the Word. . . . And the Word was made flesh, and dwelt among us, . . . full of grace and truth." — *The prologue to the Fourth Gospel.*

If we seek for a summary statement of the faith of the Protestant Church, we can scarcely do better than yet another phrase of the Reformers, " the doctrine of the Word."

The " Word of God " is God's creative activity as he relates himself to the world he has made. The New Testament asserts that the creative " Word " has become flesh in Jesus Christ and lived a life as Man among men. When Protestants speak of the Bible as the " Word " of God, they mean (at their best) that it is through the Bible that this living Word who is Jesus Christ becomes a living Word for them. The Bible is the written Word, the sermon is the preached Word, the sacraments are the enacted Word (distinctions we shall elaborate in Ch. 6) — but all these expressions of the Word serve only as ways through which *the* Word, Jesus Christ, comes alive in the hearts of men. The gospel, then, to which Protestants are called to be faithful, is Jesus Christ.

And to what this gospel means *for the Church,* we must now turn.

THE BIBLICAL UNDERSTANDING OF THE CHURCH

" The Bible is not the story of ideas about God, but the story of the people of God." — *Lesslie Newbigin.*

Exactly. There are individuals in the Bible, a fair share of heroes and an ample sprinkling of villains, but what gives significance to the Biblical story is that it is the story of the people of God. There are those who challenge God's people, trying to capture them or assimilate them or destroy them, but they never quite succeed. So the Bible is a book about God's relationship to his people — the community which becomes the Christian Church.

Where did the Church come from?

" The Church . . . is old in the sense that it is a continuation of the life of Israel, the People of God. It is new in the sense that it is founded on the revelation made through Jesus Christ of God's final purpose for mankind." — *R. Newton Flew, in* Jesus and His Church.

" Spiritually we are all Semites."
                                    — *Pope Pius XII*

It is from the Jews that we receive our faith. If you ask the question, " Where did my Church come from? " you can trace it back to the Reformation. But that, we have seen, means tracing it back to the Church described in the New Testament. Where did that come from? From a group of persons who claimed that Jesus was " the Christ," or the Anointed One sent by God. These people were Jews. (The Greek word " Christ " is the same as the Hebrew word " Messiah.") They felt that Jesus was Messiah *of the Jews*. They described themselves as " the new Israel " or the " true Israel of God." That is to say, *the early Christian community looked upon itself as the continuation and fulfillment of the Old Testament community.* So we have to push back through hundreds of years of Jewish history — back through the prophets, the years in the wilderness, the slave-labor camp in Egypt, back at least to a mysterious event on the very edge of recorded history — the " call of Abraham." Here is the moment (described in Gen., ch. 12) when the Jewish people were called into a self-conscious community, out of which the Christian community later came into being.

So it is never enough to say, " Back to the Reformation," or even, " Back to the New Testament." We must go " Back to Abraham." We could even say, " Back to the Garden of Eden," and from there, " Back to God." This would at least locate the foundation of the Church where it belongs — in God rather than man.

" The chosen people":

" How odd
Of God
To choose
The Jews."
— Housman

" But not so odd
As those who choose
The Jewish God
And spurn the Jews."
— Anonymous

Many people are affronted by the claim of the Jews to be
" the chosen people." It *is* a strange claim. They were a tiny
group of people, tucked off in a corner of the ancient world,
always overrun by stronger nations. Stranger still, they always
seemed to be denying the God who had " chosen " them. In
the pungent language of the King James Version, they " went
a whoring after other gods." How odd, indeed, that God
should choose them!

Why did he? The answer is a startling one:

> " It was not because you were more in number than
> any other people that the LORD set his love upon you and
> chose you, for you were the fewest of all peoples; but it
> is because the LORD loves you . . . that the LORD has
> brought you out with a mighty hand." — *Deut.* 7:7, 8.

It is simply because God loves this people that he chooses
them. They are not " worthy," but he loves them anyhow.
They may not " live up to expectations," but he will not desert
them. They may fail him, but he will not fail them.

And why? Not in order to shower favors upon them. No,
*the Jews are " chosen " not for special privilege but for special
responsibility.* They are to be " a light unto the Gentiles." What
is true for them is to become true for all peoples. This is a
staggering responsibility, and through much of their history
the Jews tried to bow out from under it. For it meant not an
easing, but a multiplying, of their burdens.

What God *did* in choosing them was to enter into an agree-
ment. This agreement is known in the Bible as a " covenant."
Our word " testament " is a rather poor English equivalent.
The Old and New " Testaments " could be spoken of with
greater accuracy as the Old and New " Covenants " or " Agree-
ments " between God and his people. The substance of the
" Old Covenant " (described in the events at the foot of Mt.
Sinai in Exodus) was that the Jews would be God's people,

serving him alone, while God, on his side, would be their God. "So shall you be my people, and I will be your God," it was later summarized (Jer. 11:4).

Now in ordinary covenants or agreements, if one side broke the agreement, the other side was released from obligation. Again and again the Jewish people were faithless to their promises. Again and again God remained faithful to his promise. This is perhaps the main theme of the Bible: the faithfulness of God in spite of the faithlessness of his people.

In the prophet Jeremiah a new concept of the covenant emerges. It is not based on rules and regulations, as the earlier covenant was; this new covenant God will put "in their inward parts, and write it in their hearts." It will be a possibility because God forgives:

> "They shall all know me, from the least of them unto the greatest of them, saith the Lord: for I will forgive their iniquity, and I will remember their sin no more." — *Jer. 31:34.*

This remains a hope for the future, which the New Testament transforms into a reality for the present.

It becomes clear with the passage of time that not all the Jews can live up to this high calling. There develops the notion of a "remnant," through whom the task of being "a light unto the Gentiles" shall be carried out. The nation may be sent into exile, but at least "a remnant will return," and God's work carried to completion through them. Scholars have conflicting views as to just who constitutes this remnant. One recent view suggests that the remnant was progressively narrowed down from the nation to a few, and finally to one man, Jesus, and that in the Christian community the size of the remnant began to increase again, and shall do so until all men are brought into subjection to Christ. It is the task of the remnant to remain true and faithful to God's will, come what may. This is one way to understand the task of the Church today, when it is such a minority as to seem insignificant.

Interlude: on not being too " romantic"
about the Early Church:

A FACT:
" Movies about a Christian hero
    Getting burned by a Roman Nero
Seem to attract widespread attention
Especially so in the third dimension."

A REFLECTION UPON THE FACT:
" The appeal of the films
    Does not inspire
Modern Christians
    To brave the fire." — *Saint Hereticus*.

One way to look at the " people of God " in the New Testa-ment is to see them as this remnant. But let us be careful. Christians are apt to get romantic about the " Early Church," and assume that all that is needed to solve our present prob-lems is " to be like the early Christians."

This is sheer sentimentality. The early Christians were as human as twentieth-century Christians. The term " saints " never referred to people who had reached moral perfection, but to the forgiven sinners who constituted the believing commu-nity. Forgiven, yes, with lives transformed by the redeeming power of God in Christ — but still falling. Paul's Corinthian correspondence sets the record straight. " Now that you are Christians," he seems to be saying, " for heaven's sake try to be as good as the pagans are." He scolds them for quarreling, boasting, jealousy, strife, incest, homosexuality, robbery, adultery, lust, idol worship, and for getting drunk — on the Communion wine!

But this only makes more remarkable what God accomplished through such people. It is a high tribute to his power that he could do so much with such unpromising material, and make of them the " people of God," in whom his light shone, through whom his power acted, by whom his love was manifested, and from whom the witness to his activity comes alive today.

That much abused word " fellowship":

Today " fellowship " usually means " being chummy," the third ingredient of the promise of " food, fun, and . . ."

Yet the word must be reclaimed. For it is the closest equivalent we have for the Greek *koinonia,* which describes the Early Church and means such things as sharing, togetherness, participation, mutual concern. It is God's gift; Paul blesses the Church in terms of " the grace of the Lord Jesus Christ and the love of God and the *koinonia* of the Holy Spirit " (II Cor. 13:14). This *koinonia* is a fact. We see it stemming from a handful of people in Jerusalem and Galilee, spreading out to Damascus, Ephesus, Corinth, Athens, Rome, with a vigor that is almost unbelievable. Let us look at some of the things that characterized this New Testament *koinonia,* and must always characterize the life of the Church.

The Church as created by the "good news":

" The preaching of the Early Christian Church was not an argument for the existence of God nor an admonition to follow the dictates of some common human conscience. . . . It was primarily a simple recital of the great events connected with the historical appearance of Jesus Christ and a confession of what had happened to the community of disciples." — *H. Richard Niebuhr.*

The Christian Church is a response to the " good news " of God, proclaimed and enacted by Jesus Christ. Strictly speaking, it is not only a response to the gospel, it is a *part* of the gospel, since God desires not only to save men but to have them in fellowship with one another.

The content of this gospel is found in many places in the New Testament. In fact, it *is* the New Testament. Paul tells the Corinthians about the gospel which he " received," and found to be true for himself, in his contact with the Christian community. The heart of it was that " Christ died for our sins in accordance with the scriptures, that he was buried, that he was raised on the third day in accordance with the scriptures, and that he appeared " to many people, and finally to Paul himself. " So," he says, " we preach." (I Cor. 15:3–5, 11.) In Romans he states it by saying " that Jesus is Lord and . . . that God raised him from the dead " (Rom. 10:8, 9).*

* There are elaborations in the sermons in The Acts, which Prof. C. H. Dodd has summarized:

1. The age of fulfillment has dawned. The Messianic age for which the people of God had waited so long has come.

2. This age has been ushered in by the ministry of Jesus, particularly by his death and resurrection.

3. God has exalted this Jesus to his right hand, so that he is the risen Lord in glory.

4. The Holy Spirit in the Church is the sign of the present power and glory of Christ.

5. The Messianic age will shortly reach its consummation in Christ's return.

6. Because of these things, believers are to repent, be baptized and received into the fellowship of the Church.

How would we translate this message (including the footnote) for our own day? The "good news" is still the good news today. It tells us that God, who acted in many events in Israel's history, acted in a decisive manner by sending Jesus Christ into the world. This Jesus is not just another man or prophet. He is the risen and exalted Lord of Life to whom men are to give their allegiance and loyalty. His reality is manifested in the Spirit-filled life of the community, and, as he has made himself known once, finally by the power of God he will become "all in all." He represents the gift of God's outgoing love, expressing itself toward men, and the proper response is found in a breaking with the past, and living in company with those who share the same faith.

The paraphrase is inadequate. But regardless of paraphrase, the central fact which will not be stifled is, "Jesus is Lord." Jesus is the one to whom supreme allegiance is to be given. God is no longer "aloof" or far away from men; he has identified himself with their lot in Jesus of Nazareth. By responding in faith (i.e., commitment) the life of the believer is transformed and reconstituted afresh in community with other believers. This is the destiny of men — the "new humanity" which is seen in foretaste in the Christian Church.

The Church as one, in fulfilling the promises to Israel:

The Church was one before it was many.

—*P. T. Forsyth.*

The Jews in Old Testament times gathered together in assembly or meeting (their word was *qahal*). When the Old Testament was translated into Greek, the word *ecclesia* was used (meaning those who are "called out"), a word that describes the "chosen people" rather well. All the things that were true about Israel as the chosen people become true for the Christian Church. The first "Christians" were all Jews. Many of them felt that theirs should be a fellowship only for Jews. There were some fights over this. A group in Jerusalem wanted the formula "Jew first — then Christian." Another group pressed for the inclusion of Gentiles without demanding that they become Jews first. The victory of the latter group was significant. It meant that the Christian Church did not become a Jewish sect, but became a fellowship to which anyone could belong. The extent of this oneness can be measured by the fact that Gentile Christians in Corinth soon gave up hard-earned cash to help Jewish Christians in Jerusalem.

The New Testament Church possessed another kind of unity. One cannot speak of New Testament "churches," as though there were different ones in Jerusalem, Ephesus, and Corinth. In P. T. Forsyth's figure, these were but "outcroppings" of the one great Church which underlay them all. The church worshiping in Corinth was basically the same church as was worshiping in Jerusalem or Rome. "Denominations" would have been unintelligible to a first-century Christian.

The Church as the embodiment of the "new covenant":

"Our sufficiency is from God, who has qualified us to be ministers of a *new covenant*." — *All by Paul, excepting the italics.*

The use of Jesus' language at the Last Supper is significant. "This cup," he says, "is the *new covenant* in my blood," (I Cor. 11:25) which means that by his death the new covenant will be established. The new covenant which Jeremiah had promised is now to become real. The meal dramatizes in advance what does become a reality through Jesus' death and resurrection. For it *was* those events which did " bring home " to people the fact that God had entered into a new agreement with them, based on the enactment of his forgiving love.

The Church as created by the resurrection:

" If Christ has not been raised, then our preaching is in vain and your faith is in vain." — *Paul, on the heart of the faith.*

The impact of Jesus' crucifixion was shattering. Some of the disciples fled the city. Others gathered together — but behind locked doors, as they so candidly tell us, because they were afraid that they would be crucified too.

And then came the world-shaking experience that Jesus who had been dead was no longer dead. They knew that he was alive and with them. They could not always describe just how he appeared to them. Sometimes they felt that they must not touch him, while at other times he was so earthy that they could offer him boiled fish. But that he was alive and in their midst, they had no doubt. This faith transformed them from people who were scared to death into people who were willing to go the length and breadth of the Roman Empire, proclaiming that God was victor over sin and death, and that they could be in constant relationship with a risen Lord.

There is a monastic order today called " The Community of the Resurrection." It would be a good name for the whole Church.

The Church as based on the activity of the Holy Spirit:

" The Holy Spirit — why, that is what they talk about in the ' fringe sects,' not in proper congregations affiliated with the National Council of the Churches of Christ in the United States of America." — *Henry Sloane Coffin, paraphrasing the attitude of the typical modern congregation.*

There is a sense in which lack of talk about the Holy Spirit is perfectly proper. There is nothing more mysterious than God manifesting himself *right now* in people's lives as transforming power. To claim too much understanding of such a God is spiritual arrogance. And yet, Christians cannot be silent at this point. As we read The Acts of the Apostles (which might better be named The Acts of the Holy Spirit) we find that the early Christians attribute their power and energy to this same Holy Spirit.

They do not just talk about God the Father Almighty, known to them in their Jewish heritage; nor do they just talk about Jesus Christ, crucified, buried, and risen from the dead; they talk also about God, the Holy Spirit, actively present in their lives, giving them vitality and courage, putting words into their mouths, making it possible for them to cure the sick, heal the diseased, transform lives.

They trace their inception as a self-conscious community to that strange event we know as Pentecost, described in Acts, ch. 2. The disciples are gathered together in a room, waiting. They do not know what they are to do. And then something happens. A kind of energy is released. They feel the active presence of God in their midst. They realize that the One has come whom Jesus promised — the Comforter, the Paraclete, the Counselor. And they go forth with power and conviction.

The Church is not maintained by the works of men or the endeavors of Ladies' Aids or the bustle of parsons. It is sustained — and reformed — by the power of God at work in the Holy Spirit. The Church is the place where the Spirit dwells.

Men find him there, and he uses those men so that he may find others there and elsewhere. Only in terms of his activity can the Church be understood.

We are not to glorify the early Christians, but Him whom they glorified. As they had " one Lord, one faith, one baptism," so do we. As they proclaimed that " Jesus Christ is Lord," so do we. As they failed to live as they should, we do likewise. But as God forgave, restored, and empowered them through the life in the Spirit, he does so likewise to us.

4

WHAT, THEN, IS THE CHURCH?
... With a Further Exercise in Vocabulary

"The Church is first and foremost a divine reality. This distinguishes it from all other realities. . . . For those who, by faith, affirm it and belong to it, it is the whole family of God in heaven and on earth, it is the work of God in the world." — *Professor J. Coert Rylaarsdam.*

It is time to pull our lines together, and summarize ways in which the word "church" has been used by Christians.

The commonest definition is that the church is *a local congregation,* housed in a specific building. The church is the place you go to on Sunday, or the building you pass on Saturday (and perhaps on Sunday) on your way to the golf course. It has a minister, an organ, some bizarre windows, and a mortgage.

But it is also a place where people have been sustained in times of tragedy, where they have prayed to God and felt his presence, where they have gone to offer themselves up in service for others. The Church may be much more than a local gathering of people, but it must always be at least that. No "invisible" Church is worth talking about unless it receives

on earth to whom men must give allegiance. To the Catholic contention, *"Ubi Petrus ibi ecclesia"* (Where Peter — or his successor — is, there is the Church), the Protestant stoutly replies, *"Ubi Christus ibi ecclesia"* (Where Christ is, there is the Church).

The Church as the "Bride of Christ"

"From heaven he came and sought her
To be His holy Bride."

The hymn now describes the Church as Christ's bride. The figure is infrequent in the New Testament, but it recurs often in the history of the Church. Feminine readers will not like the figure very much, because it is a symbol of obedience. Just as the wife was supposed to be obedient to the husband in Biblical times, so the Church is to be obedient to Christ, who is the "head of the household." The figure thus reminds us of the subservience of the Church to her master. The Church acts in his name, not in her own; her message is of him, not of herself.

The Church as Dependent Upon the "Work" of Christ

"With His own blood He bought her
And for her life He died."

The mention of "blood" strikes most modern readers as repulsive. And yet Christian faith asserts that in the death of Jesus something "happened" which affected the relationship of God and men. In order to demonstrate God's love, Christ was willing to die that men might know the extent of this love. Since he was killed by sinful men, we can say that in the crucifixion, men's sin and God's love were locked in mortal combat. And Christian faith, linking the cross with the resurrection, asserts that the powers of sin and death could not hold Christ captive, but that through him God overcame those powers. It is out of this triumph that the Christian Church was born.

Thus it is a sober reporting of the facts to say that Christ "bought" the Church with his blood (i.e., with his very "life") and that when he died he did so for "her life," so that the Church might exist to witness to the victorious God. Because of his death, the Church lives.

The Church as the "People of God"

" Elect from every nation,
Yet one o'er all the earth,
Her charter of salvation
One Lord, one faith, one birth."

We have seen how God chose Israel as his special people, electing her to be "a light unto the Gentiles," and how the Early Christian Church felt herself the inheritor of this task and looked upon herself as the "new Israel" to evangelize all nations. We have seen how "her charter of salvation" is faith in one Lord, Jesus Christ. Later we shall discuss "one birth" (baptism).

It is true at all times that the Church is never "chosen" because of her greatness, but simply because God loves her, in spite of her brokenness, arrogance, and sin. The claim to be the "people of God" leads, not to pride, but to repentance, and the promised newness of life which can flow from God's mercy. This means that the people of God must not only proclaim the good news, but embody it in their own life. If God forgives them, they are to forgive one another. If God loves them in spite of their unworthiness, then they are to " love the brethren " in spite of the brethren's unworthiness. If God gives good gifts to them, then they are to share those gifts with one another and all mankind. The people of God must therefore always be a missionary people, an evangelizing people, seeking to engraft the gospel in the hearts of all men and nations, that the God to whom they give allegiance may become the God to whom all men give allegiance.

The Church as a Sacramental Community

" One holy Name she blesses,
Partakes one holy food."

" Protestants " often leave the sacramental side of the Church's life to " Catholics " and assume that there is something suspicious about the whole business. As we shall see in Ch. 6, this is a betrayal of the Reformers, for whom " partaking of one holy food " was the highest and most joyful moment in the entire life of the Church.

The Church itself can be sacramental of the divine love poured out for mankind, as it concerns itself in love with the lives of men. It can be a place where the deep experiences of human life are brought into the presence of God. The individual within the community who knows that he is forgiven by God may be more ready to forgive his neighbor; and the one who, within the sacramental fellowship, has been forgiven by his neighbor, may find in that a deeper knowledge of what God's forgiveness is. The joining of two people in marriage is given a sacramental character as it is blessed by the Church, under God. The fact of death is seen in the light of God and the assurance of " the life everlasting." All the high moments of life can become " windows to eternity," or sacraments, as they are related to the life of the Church.

The Church as a Foretaste of the Kingdom of God

> " *And to one hope she presses,*
> *With every grace endued.*"

> " In Protestant churches
> There's been a dearth
> Of living as ' strangers
> And pilgrims on earth.' "
> — *Saint Hereticus*

And it's a great loss. For the Church should look forward to the consummation of " one hope." It should be a " pilgrim people," a band that is on the march, its face set toward the coming Kingdom of God, not as something that will be " built " by muscular Christians, but as a gift that God will give in his own good time. Christians live as " strangers and pilgrims on earth." They look " forward to the city which has foundations, whose builder and maker is God." They have not received what was promised, " but having seen it and greeted it from afar," they " make it clear that they are seeking a homeland." (See Heb., ch. 11.)

To borrow a phrase from Paul, they are " a colony of heaven " (Moffatt). A colony exists far away from the homeland, but the members give allegiance not just to the colony, but chiefly to the homeland. And the Church as a " colony of heaven " is thus a foretaste or " earnest " of what is one day to be true for all.

This sounds strange, and yet this is the dimension of the Church's life that distinguishes it from all other groups. Christians are reminded at the Lord's Supper that they show forth the Lord's death " till he come." " The return of Christ " is a difficult symbol in any case, but at least it stands for the fact that history — and the life of the Church — moves toward *him,* rather than toward chaos or the devil. The Church then must live expectantly, waiting in hope and promise for God's activity in history. It lives between the time when God appeared in Christ and the time when all things shall be in subjection unto him.

The Church as the Communion of Saints

> *" Yet she on earth hath union*
> *With God the Three in One,*
> *And mystic sweet communion*
> *With those whose rest is won."*

" O God, our heavenly Father, who hast given us the blessed assurance that the dead as well as the living are in Thy care; we give Thee thanks for all dear and loved ones who have passed away from our earthly fellowship. *Keep us, with them, in the everlasting fellowship of Thy Church,* and bring us at last, cleansed and purified, to the glory and beauty of Thine eternal presence; through Jesus Christ our Lord. Amen." — *A prayer from* The Book of Common Order of the Church of Scotland.

Here is another emphasis for Protestants to recover. The " communion of saints " is the ultimate expression of the *koinonia* we talked about in Ch. 3. It has two significant dimensions.

It refers to the fellowship of Christians in all places where the Christian community exists. When you break bread at the

Lord's Table in Omaha, you are in communion with Christians in Chartres, Bangalore, and even Kansas City. The partitions, the divisions, are broken down. And the communion of saints is very real for those who pray together, who engage in acts of love and service for one another, and who share deep sorrow and deep joy.

Yet there is a further dimension to the communion of saints, for Christians claim to be in a communion that transcends time. In their intermittent worship on earth they join in the unending life of praise which the redeemed in heaven offer to God. They unite " with angels and archangels and *all the company of heaven* " in uttering the praises of God. In prayer, Christians come close to God and to all who are close to God, whether alive or not. Those who have died do not " leave the Church " but become those in the Church who have an unclouded vision of the God who is God both of the dead and of the living.

This cannot be described in cold type or even in warm prose. But it can be a part of the experience of any of the people of God. Those who have passed through " the valley of the shadow of death " themselves will know it best.

WHAT ABOUT THE ROMAN CATHOLICS?
... With an Appeal for Charity and Firmness All Around

"The Church is called CATHOLIC, or universal; because there could not be two or three churches, without Christ being divided, which is impossible." — *John Calvin, a Protestant if there ever was one.*

The phrase "the Holy Catholic Church" makes many Protestants bristle. To them "Catholic" is a fighting word.

On reclaiming the word " Catholic ":

"I am a High Church Presbyterian Reformed Protestant Catholic." — *Alexander Miller, an ordained minister of the Presbyterian Church of New Zealand.*

As a matter of fact, "the Holy Catholic Church" *is* the Church in which Protestants believe. The word "catholic" means "all-embracing," "universal," "whole." There is a *part* of the Holy Catholic Church that gives its allegiance to the bishop of Rome; hence it is called (quite rightly) the "Roman" Catholic Church. But it has no rightful monopoly on the word "catholic." Any Christian who gives his allegiance to Jesus Christ as Lord and Savior, with all which that implies, believes in the Catholic Church. It would thus be quite proper for a person to refer to himself as a " Protestant Catholic," or a " Reformed Catholic," i.e., one whose membership in the Holy Catholic Church is guided by fidelity to the Scriptural witness to Christ. The full meaning of " Protestant " thus implies " being part of the Catholic Church, Reformed." As a matter of fact, the Westminster Confession of Faith, in Ch. XXV, " Of the Church," describes the Church as " catholic." The word " protestant " does not occur at all.

A recent book is brilliantly titled *The Catholicity of Protestantism*. Since " catholicity " means preserving the wholeness of the gospel, it can be claimed that this is precisely the heritage to which Protestantism tries to be faithful. There could be nothing more authentically " catholic " than the Reformation, calling the Church to return to the living Christ and the whole gospel.

The Protestant–Roman Catholic issue today:

But there are still difficulties between Protestants and Roman Catholics. Let the issue of a parochial versus a public school be raised in a community, let Congress discuss a bill for Federal aid to education, let the President propose an ambassador to the Vatican, and immediately the battle lines are drawn. Why should this be so?

A " good " Roman Catholic: My Church is the Church that Jesus Christ founded. For fifteen hundred years this Church represented Christ on earth. Then, with the " Protestant revolt," all sorts of new groups sprang up, pretending (quite falsely) to be the true Church. Since the Catholic Church has the truth, all that helps her helps the cause of Christ. Whatever thwarts her, thwarts the cause of Christ. Thus I must work for my Church, send my children to her schools, and dedicate myself to her advancement and gain, so that the Kingdom of Christ may advance and gain. I become a trifle edgy when attempts are made to limit my Church and thus to stifle truth.

A " good " Protestant: I too believe that Jesus Christ founded the Church, and that it must be faithful to the good news he brought. When it has not been, God has raised up reformers (not " revolters ") to call the Church back to him. I cannot feel that God works only through a part of Christendom, and since I know that all men can err, I must allow for truth and error in every part of the Church — my own included, the Roman Catholic branch included.

This means that no one segment of the Church should have rights denied to others, for the abuse of power is a temptation on every level. Thus I become edgy when attempts are made by Roman Catholics to gain special privileges or to gain power that will be used to stifle my religious freedom.

Both spokesmen have been consistent with their convictions. But feelings often run high. And, since we are speaking to Protestants, let us characterize some Protestant forms of anti-Catholicism.

Types of " Anti-Catholicism "

1. *The " if they're for it I'm agin' it" type.* This " protestant " uses all his energy being against Catholicism. His creed is negative: he does not believe in the saints, he does not believe in the pope — he opposes everything the Catholics are for. He knows all about the Inquisition and can quote all the unwise things that members of the

hierarchy say. He knows the worst; he will not listen to the best.*

But there are embarrassing skeletons in Protestant closets too. Catholics have no monopoly on sin.

2. *The " when they get to be the majority they'll destroy our freedom " approach.* This person has data on the " Catholic " countries, like Spain, Italy, and Colombia. Here Protestants are denied many rights which Catholics have and are often persecuted if they try to evangelize. The inference is that if Catholics get to be the majority in America the same thing will happen.

In predominantly Catholic countries, Protestants often *do* suffer for their minority status. This has been true in Spain and Colombia. Furthermore, many Catholics assert (see Ryan and Boland, *Catholic Principles of Politics*) that if Catholics were in an overwhelming majority in America, they would deny certain rights to Protestants. On the other side, there are Catholic writers who do not accept this conclusion. But it is hard to know how much weight they carry in the total Catholic picture.

* Much of his ammunition comes from the writings of Paul Blanshard, who compares Roman Catholicism with Russian Communism, describes it as a totalitarian regime, out to stifle individualism, thwart liberty, etc. Blanshard has amassed impressive documentation for many of his charges. But his tone and manner are so ardently " anti-Catholic " that the force of his argument is often lost. One wonders whether it would be worse to live in a country dominated by the Catholic mentality Blanshard describes, or the Blanshard mentality he embodies. His writings have so alienated sincere Catholics that it has become immeasurably harder to engage in creative interfaith communication.

3. *The " vast monolithic structure " approach.* This person talks about the " Catholic vote," is sure that there are no matters on which Catholics disagree, and that the people always do just what the priest says.

On matters of faith and morals, clearly defined, Catholics *must* agree fully with what the Church says. But beyond that there are wide differences of opinion. Some Catholic theologians are Thomists; others, Augustinians. Some Catholics like the Dodgers; others, the Giants. Some Catholics are Democrats; others, Republicans. The notion that there is an undeviating " Catholic mind " is simply not true.

4. *The " Catholicism is clericalism " approach.* In its more sophisticated form this position registers a complaint (which most Protestants would claim as legitimate) that the Catholic hierarchy is a disturbing " power bloc," able to influence public life to its own ends.

On a less sophisticated level, this attitude is roughly equivalent to " Catholicism is like the priest in our community." The Protestant knows that the priest (*a*) promotes bingo games, (*b*) uses wine in the Mass, (*c*) believes that Roman Catholicism is the only true faith, and (*d*) is raising funds for a parochial school. So the Protestant reasons that *all* Catholics are, respectively, (*a*) gamblers, (*b*) drunkards, (*c*) think all Protestants are going to hell, and (*d*) oppose American democracy.

With regard to the more sophisticated form, more later. With regard to the less sophisticated form, no comment necessary.

A Deeper Level of Disagreement

Some Protestants believe that at certain points Roman Catholic faith departs from Christian faith, and that out of faithfulness to the gospel, they must oppose it.

EXAMPLE ONE: The pope is able to speak " infallibly " (i.e., without possibility of human error), on matters of faith and morals.

The Protestant rejects this belief. All human understanding of God is distorted by human sin, and to claim an exception to this is to elevate the exception to a place which belongs to God alone. Behind all the excessive language of the Reformers about the papacy as " anti-Christ " (the tone of which modern Protestants must disavow), there was this important truth — that the claims made for the papacy were claims which could be made for none save God.

EXAMPLE TWO: The Dogma of the Assumption, the recent " infallible " pronouncement of the pope, that Mary's body was not received into the grave, but raised up by God uncorrupted into heaven.

Why does the Protestant reject this belief? Because (*a*) there is no Scriptural basis for it, (*b*) it has not been part of the " catholic " faith of Christendom, but is a relatively recent " importation." (Saint Thomas Aquinas, the " official " Roman Catholic theologian, rejected the belief as untenable.) (*c*) More important is the implication of the belief, which makes Mary virtually coredeemer of mankind with Jesus. The belief seems to minimize the unique and saving work of Jesus Christ on behalf of mankind, and to suggest that he needs assistance.

Thus in both cases it is because of their profound faith in

God and in Christ that Protestants feel bound to reject these doctrines.

What Are Protestants to Do?

What can be done to meet this situation creatively? There are certainly no panaceas. But there are at least four areas in which the Protestant has a responsibility.

1. The first thing he must do is to *understand his own faith better*. Only if the Protestant knows whereon he stands can he assess another viewpoint with integrity. What it means to understand Protestant faith need not be spelled out here. The whole purpose of the series, of which this book is one, is to do just that. The Protestant must love God with all his *mind,* as well as with his heart and soul and strength, if he is truly to follow the command of Christ.

2. The Protestant must *understand Roman Catholicism better than he does*. It is not enough to read what angry Protestant writers say about Roman Catholics. We would hardly feel that our faith had been adequately explained to a Roman Catholic, if he read only an interpretation by an angry non-Protestant. In order to understand Roman Catholicism, the Protestant must try to see it as a Roman Catholic himself would see it. This will never be *completely* possible, just as no Roman Catholic could ever see Protestantism completely from the inside. But the effort must be made.

Here are two instances of common Protestant misunderstanding of Catholicism:

INSTANCE ONE: Belief in the infallibility of the pope does *not* mean that the pope is perfect, or that *everything* he says and writes is infallible. It is only when certain conditions are fulfilled (the pope must be speaking ex cathedra, i.e., from the bishop's chair in St. Peter's in Rome about a matter of faith or morals) that the utterance is held to be infallible. This does not apply to the papal encyclicals (letters to the faithful). The only utterance that is beyond all doubt " infallible " is the Dogma of the Assumption, proclaimed in 1950.

INSTANCE TWO: Many Protestants believe that the Catholic Church consigns all non-Catholics to hell, and that only Catholics get to heaven. Catholics do hold that those who know Catholicism to be the truth and still reject it will not be saved. But Catholicism does not draw up a list of such individuals. It refuses to identify a single inhabitant of hell, since the " uncovenanted mercies of God " may reach out beyond what men can define or understand.

The study of Roman Catholicism will not convince the Protestant that it is the truth. But it should help the Protestant to be able to say, " I can begin to understand how Roman Catholics can believe such and such, even though I never could myself." This is clear gain.

3. The third ingredient calls for *the exercise of that rare virtue, charity*. Karl Adam, in *One and Holy,* urges this upon his Roman Catholic brethren, and the Protestant must carry his own weight in this endeavor. Difficult though it may be for him, the Protestant must try to see Roman Catholicism in the light of its best exponents, rather than its worst. There *is* greatness in the Roman Catholic tradition, and it should be appreciated.

The Protestant should be thankful that the Roman Catholic Church has given us such consecrated men of God as Baron von Hügel, one of the most gracious Christian " saints " of the twentieth century; that there are Roman Catholic novelists like

Graham Greene writing about the grace of God; that there are philosophers like Jacques Maritain who write with deep Christian concern about the spiritual vacuum in modern life. Not all Roman Catholics are like certain cardinals who so constantly offend Protestant consciences.

Again, the Protestant should remember that if there is an emphasis in Christendom upon the sacredness of the high moments of life — birth, confirmation, marriage, and death — it is in part because of the ongoing influence of the sacraments of the Roman Church through the centuries. Protestants need to be reminded of the creativity of the " liturgical movement " in modern Roman Catholicism, a kind of reform movement *within* the Church, which is stressing the importance of lay participation in worship, so that the Mass is not just a " show " that people go to watch, and which is recalling Catholics to an understanding of the Church as the mystical Body of Christ.*

The Protestant must assess Roman Catholicism by the same standard as he would want his own faith assessed — by the best that it has produced, rather than the worst.

4. But the *Protestant must combine an attitude of charity with an attitude of firmness*. Charity by itself can lead to sentimentality, firmness by itself can lead to harshness.

Protestants need to stand firm at a number of points. In connection with matters of faith (such as papal infallibility and the assumption of the Virgin, mentioned earlier), Protestants cannot act as though these beliefs do not " make any differ-

---

* Modern Catholic architecture is beginning to bring the altar down from the east end of the church and put it at the " crossing," so that the people of God may gather *around* the Lord's Table (ironically enough, at the very time " liturgically minded " Protestants are taking their authentic Communion Table, shoving it against the east wall, making an altar of it, and thus repudiating their Reformation heritage — a disease known in some Protestant circles as " chancelitis ").

ence." They do. They change the whole substance of the gospel. Authentic Biblical faith must be proclaimed by Protestants in their stead.

Protestants need to stand firm in the face of some types of "political" Catholicism. This does not mean opposing statesmen who are Catholics. But it does mean that there may be issues when the lines will be drawn. If, for example, Roman Catholic pressures are exerted on the State Department to keep Protestant missionaries out of South America, this must be opposed. The Protestant must be sure of his facts, and then act through political channels, rather than beat the drum for anti-Catholic sentiment.

Protestants need to stand firm about Catholic misrepresentations of Protestantism. Attention has been called to Protestant misunderstanding of Roman Catholicism. But the shoe fits on the other foot too. There have been Catholic treatments of the Reformation that were defamations of the word "scholarship," and Catholic lives of the Reformers that were little more than falsehood and innuendo. When Catholics assert that Reformed Protestants do not believe in the "real presence" of Christ in the Lord's Supper, or that Protestantism was founded by "mere men" while Roman Catholicism was founded by Christ, or that Luther "left the Church" so he could get married — then the Protestant must be firm in correcting such distortions.

The Protestant's firmness does not consist in stubborn resistance to Rome. His *real* firmness consists in the strength with which he make his own witness. Long ago, in a time of crisis, Martin Luther said: "Here I stand. I can do no other. God help me."

That must be the firmness of the Protestant.

CHAPTER

6

THE SHARED LIFE OF THE PEOPLE OF GOD
. . . Or, the Church Says *Yes* and *No*

" All people that on earth do dwell,
   Sing to the Lord with cheerful voice;
Him serve with mirth, His praise forthtell,
   Come ye before Him and rejoice."
        — *A metrical version of Psalm 100 by William*
       Kethe, in the Anglo-Genevan Psalter

The thing most characteristic of the " people of God " is that with more or less fidelity they obey the command, " Come ye before Him." They may forget to come before him ". . . and rejoice," and they may not always sing " with cheerful voice," or serve him " with mirth," but " getting together on Sunday morning " is certainly the most obvious thing they do. If they took seriously what went on " at 11 o'clock on Sunday morning," the whole life of the Church would be transformed.

The recovery of a heritage:

Most Protestant worship is sheer chaos. The service jumps from hymn to solo to prayer to Bible-reading to announcements to longer prayer to longer talk (not always worthy of the name of " sermon ").

Does Protestantism have a heritage of worship it could recover, as well as a heritage of belief? The answer is yes, although this does not imply doing things in church " just because the Reformers did." Calvin wore a hat in church, not because Scripture demanded it but because the church had (*a*) drafts and (*b*) pigeons.

But a heritage can be appropriated creatively. And there are elements in the worship of the Reformers that represent the " recovery of the gospel " just as forcefully as their theology did. Let us look at some of these, as aids in seeing what the shared life of the people of God might be today.

1. The Center of Worship Is God and Not Man

" Know that the Lord is God indeed;
Without our aid He did us make;
We are His flock, He doth us feed,
And for His sheep He doth us take."
                    — *William Kethe* (**again**)

" Yesterday Mr. Parker offered the finest prayer ever delivered to a Boston audience. — *A Monday morning newspaper account.*

The purpose of gathering together on Sunday morning is to praise God and to honor his name.

This note is lacking in much contemporary worship. Church services are designed to " do us good," or give us a spiritual shot in the arm. The emphasis is all upon *us*, and what we " get out of it." Now worship that does not reach the participant can be very sterile indeed. But the center of attention in true worship is to be not us but God. Not our state of mind, but his glory, comes first. The significant thing is that God is honored through song, prayer, giving, and attentiveness to the hearing of his Word. The worshiping community gathers to give him " the praise due unto his name." A prayer is not delivered to a " Boston audience," it is offered to God the Father Almighty.

The point is open to misunderstanding. It is not a plea for coldness and " lack of relevance." It is a plea for a proper center of worship — God. When this has been established, then everything is relevant. For example:

Reformed worship characteristically began with the words, " Our help is in the name of the Lord, who made heaven and earth." And to that Lord the congregation immediately turned in corporate confession of sin. Really to believe in " the Lord, who made heaven and earth " is to be aware of how far one is from doing his will. This is sin — which must be confessed. It was. And then, pronounced by the minister, came the gracious words of the " Assurance of Pardon," the promise that to those who confessed their sin, God was faithful and just to forgive them their sin. This was not, and is not, cold irrelevance. It is placing worshipers in the only proper relationship to God — that of forgiven sinners to a forgiving Father.

2. The Significance of the Christian Heritage

> " For why? the Lord our God is good,
>   His mercy is forever sure;
>   His truth at all times firmly stood,
>   And shall from age to age endure."
>   — *William Kethe (once more)*

Since the Reformation was a " rediscovery of the gospel," we will see this underlined in Reformation worship, for the Reformers made use of the riches of tradition. There was, for example, a continuity with the *Hebraic past,* out of which Christendom had sprung. The hymns were metrical versions of the Psalms — the hymnbook of the Jewish temple. The benediction was often the Aaronic blessing found in the book of Numbers. The reading from the Old Testament (so notoriously absent from contemporary worship) was a reminder of the promises of God, later fulfilled in Jesus Christ, to his own people.

There was also continuity with the *Christian past*. Not only was the New Testament read, but the Reformers also used the Apostles' Creed (and others) in Sunday worship. Calvin felt that since the creeds were an offering of praise to God, they should be sung.

Such facts remind us that we never " start from scratch." We too are the inheritors of a tradition, now enriched by the Reformers, from which we should not be afraid to draw. This is one way in which we can exemplify the ongoingness of the people of God.

3. The Significance of Congregational Singing

" O enter then His gates with praise,
Approach with joy His courts unto;
Praise, laud, and bless His Name always,
For it is seemly so to do."
— *William Kethe (for the last time)*

" In singing the praises of God, we are to sing with spirit, and with the understanding also; making melody

in our hearts unto the Lord. It is also proper that we cul-
tivate some knowledge of the rules of music." — *The Di-
rectory for the Public Worship of God (1645), a product
of the Westminster Divines.*

The layman in medieval worship had become a spectator.
The Reformation made him a participant once again. One way
this was done was by praising God through song. The important thing is not that the congregation sang hymns; the important thing is the kind of hymns they sang. Again, the center
of attention was God.

There was vitality and integrity in both music and words
of Reformation hymnody. The *music* was strong and vigorous,
a reflection in human terms of the Lord God Almighty, who
was the subject of the music. Even the most debased modern
hymnbook has tunes from the Genevan Psalter and the Scot-
tish Psalter which underline the point better than any prose
description can. Here will be found " Old Hundredth " (whose
magnificent rhythm has been spoiled in modern versions of the
" Doxology "), " Old 124th," " Donne Secours," " Toulon,"
" Dundee," and many others. They are a welcome contrast to
nineteenth-century chromatic fantasies and gospel jazz hymns.
(Praising God in three-quarter time is one of the most difficult
of spiritual exercises.)

The *words* were metrical paraphrases of the psalms. This is
an unnecessary stricture on hymnody today, but modern
hymns might well be chosen on the basis of how well they reflect the spirit of the Psalmists, with their stress on the total
giving of the self to God's adoration and glorification.

4. The Centrality of the Word

" Wherever we find the Word of God surely preached
and heard, and the sacraments administered according to

the institution of Christ, there, it is not to be doubted, is a church of God." — *John Calvin, in the* Institutes.

The centrality of the Word (see Ch. 2) is emphasized in three ways:

There is *the written Word,* the Bible. The reading of the Word is a solemn and important part of every service of worship. Calvin regularly preceded it with a prayer for illumination, that the Holy Spirit who had inspired the hearts of the writers likewise inspire the hearts of the hearers, so that by his power the Biblical Word might become the very living Word of life for the worshiper.

Closely linked with the written Word is *the spoken Word,* or sermon, which attempts to make relevant a portion of the written Word. It should not be a series of snippets from *The Reader's Digest;* it should be the minister's attempt to drive home for his people the contemporary relevance of the events recounted in the Bible. So the sermon is very important. It is not the center. The center is *the enacted Word,* the Lord's Supper. The Reformed liturgies, leading to a climax in the celebration of the sacrament, make this clear. And since at no other point has Protestantism been less faithful to its heritage we must discuss this in more detail.

The significance of the sacraments:

"The highest cannot be spoken; it can only be acted." — *Goethe, who was not a Christian but is here expressing a Christian insight.*

"A sacrament is an outward and visible sign of an inward and spiritual grace." — *The common treasury of Christendom.*

Occasionally in Protestant churches, a table will be covered with a cloth and after some words have been spoken, tiny portions of bread and wine will be distributed. Or a couple will bring forward a baby, and the minister will sprinkle a few drops of water on the child's head. Presumably these events have special significance in the life of the Church.

They have. These are the " sacraments," the *enacted* Word. In Protestant faith, a sacrament is a means whereby God conveys to the believer his own presence and reality through the use of ordinary objects like water or wine or bread, which are the " signs " (outward and visible) of his " grace " (inward and spiritual). Let us look at them in turn.

" The Breaking of the Bread "

" Deck thyself, my soul, with gladness,
   Leave thy gloomy haunts of sadness;
   Come into the daylight's splendour,
   There with joy thy praises render
   Unto him whose grace unbounded
   Hath this wondrous banquet founded:
   High o'er all the heavens he reigneth
   Yet to dwell with thee he deigneth."
                    — *An old Communion hymn*

" Do this for my recalling." — *D. M. Baillie's more accurate rendering of the words of Christ often translated, " Do this in remembrance of me."*

A couple of days after Jesus' death, two men hiked from Jerusalem to Emmaus. They picked up a stranger. At supper the stranger " took the bread and blessed, and broke it, and gave it to them. And their eyes were opened and they recognized him." (Luke 24:30, 31.) They knew it was Jesus because " he was known to them in the breaking of the bread " (Luke 24:35).

This is a " preview " of what has been true for Christians ever since. As they " break bread " together, whether they call it the Lord's Supper, the Holy Communion, the Eucharist, or the Mass, they are aware of that same risen Christ in their midst. They do this " for his recalling." They may be:

sailors kneeling before a makeshift altar on the after gun turret of a destroyer escort at sea,

crowds thronging the nave of a European cathedral,

two or three folk who have braved the snow to gather in a New England chapel,

a quiet group kneeling before a kitchen table in East Berlin with a price upon their heads;

but they are all aware of the real presence of Christ in their midst. His real presence is not localized in the elements (as the Roman Catholic doctrine of transubstantiation claims) but the elements stand as the tangible evidence of this presence, as the means by which the living Christ is conveyed to them and they enter into union with him. On what basis do they approach Christ's Table?

" All that humbly put their trust in Christ, and desire his help that they may lead a holy life, all that are truly sorry for their sins and would be delivered from the burden of them, are invited and encouraged in his name to come to this sacrament."

So goes one Word of Invitation. The sacrament is not for those who are " good enough." It is for those who know that they are *not* " good enough." Participation is based on penitence rather than self-congratulation.

The service itself

" I received from the Lord what I also delivered to you, that the Lord Jesus on the night when he was betrayed took bread, and when he had given thanks, he broke it, and said, ' This is my body which is broken for you. Do this in remembrance of me.' In the same way also the cup, after supper, saying, ' This cup is the new covenant in my blood. Do this, as often as you drink it, in remembrance of me.' For as often as you eat this bread and drink the cup, you proclaim the Lord's death until he comes." — *Saint Paul's account, the earliest we possess, of the Last Supper.*

What " goes on " at a Communion service? It is modeled on the service Jesus shared with his disciples.

1. First of all, " the Lord Jesus . . . *took bread*." The minister likewise " takes " the elements, laying his hands upon them, so that they may be set apart from a common usage to a holy one.

2. Next, in Paul's account, Jesus *gives thanks*. We are similarly to approach his Table with thanksgiving. The service is often called the " Eucharist," from the Greek word for " thanksgiving." It is a resurrection feast of joy, not a wake to commemorate death.

Included within the prayer of thanksgiving is a prayer of consecration, in which the minister asks God to bless and sanctify his own gifts of bread and wine which the people have placed on Christ's Table. They are no longer to be looked upon as lifeless symbols, but as signs now vibrant with his presence. The people also pray, " We offer and present unto Thee *our-*

selves, our souls and bodies, to be a reasonable, holy, and living sacrifice."

3. After Jesus took the bread and gave thanks, *" he broke it."* The minister breaks the bread in the view of the people, as a reminder that Christ's body is a *broken* body, broken for our sakes upon the cross. The victory he achieved there over sin and death was a costly one. The actual breaking of the bread enacts this central fact. The same thing is dramatized by the pouring of the wine, representing Christ's blood (or life) which is "poured out" on our behalf.

4. Finally, Jesus gave the bread and wine to his followers, saying, "Take, eat." At this point, the pastor, ministering in Christ's name, likewise "gives" the elements to the people, who receive "the body of Christ which is broken for you," and the cup which is "the New Covenant in the blood of Christ, which is shed for many unto remission of sins." After this great gift, there is a concluding prayer of thanksgiving.

That's all.

What does it mean?

Why should this be the moment in all their existence when the people of God are most *truly* the people of God?

1. Pre-eminently, the service is *an enactment of the gospel,* that God in Christ has come to us and by his sacrificial death redeemed our lives. The Bible describes this, sermons talk about it, but the sacrament *dramatizes* it. Calvin, following Augustine, called it "the Word made *visible.*"

2. *By partaking of the elements, we indicate that we wish Christ to dwell in our hearts by faith.* At other times we may talk about our faith; here we act it out. As we take the bread and wine into our physical bodies, we are indicating by that action our wish that Christ enter into us. And the sacrament itself is God's promise that he does.

3. Not only are we joined with him, but *we are also united in a new way with our fellow believers*. Here is when *koinonia*, or fellowship, is most real. We are not just individuals before God, but we are a community united together before God. This being so, as Calvin puts it,

> " it is impossible for us to wound, despise, reject, injure, or in any way to offend one of our brethren, but we, at the same time, wound, despise, reject, injure, and offend Christ in him. . . . We have not discord with our brethren without being, at the same time, at variance with Christ. . . . We cannot love Christ without loving him in our brethren." — *Calvin,* Institutes, *IV, xvii, 38.*

Here is where " the communion of saints " (see Ch. 4) is most real. As the Eucharistic prayer reminds us, we are " in the communion of all the faithful in heaven and on earth." We are not just " present company " praising God; we are joining in the perpetual chorus of praise that is offered to God by " all the company of heaven." Since God is " the King of all creation," his children in all of creation can be one at this particular moment.

4. The service underlines *the significance of our everyday life*. We bring bread and wine (God's gifts in the first place), the symbols of our earthly toil, and get back Christ. God uses common things as channels of his revelation. The act of eating can make God more real than a stained-glass window. The act of drinking can make God more real than a fifty-voice robed choir. There is nothing too ordinary to be used by him. All of life is sacred and holy.

No wonder that Calvin and Knox wanted weekly celebration of the sacrament. No wonder modern worship is impoverished when it is celebrated only four times a year.

The Sacrament of Baptism

" Baptism is not . . . primarily for the individual, nor
for the family, but for the Church, to confess before God
and man the Word of Regeneration." — *P. T. Forsyth, a
" high church" Congregationalist.*

If the Lord's Supper is mystifying, the sacrament of Baptism
(particularly infant Baptism) is even more so. Why is sprinkling water on a person's head so important?

Since it is the Protestant claim that only the two sacraments
of Baptism and the Lord's Supper have Biblical sanction, it
will be well to get the New Testament material before us.

1. Jesus himself was baptized, and his disciples baptized in
   his name. (Matt. ch. 3; 28:18, 19.)
2. The early Christians designated Baptism as the mode of
   entrance into their fellowship, and they baptized because
   of the command of Christ. (Acts 2:38; 8:14-16; 19:2-5.)
3. Baptism was a way of being identified with Christ, both
   in his death and resurrection. (Gal. 3:25-27; Eph. 4:4-6;
   Col. 2:12.)
4. Baptism was probably adult Baptism, but soon the children of believers were baptized also.

We have described the sacraments as enactments of the gospel. How does the sacrament of adult Baptism " act out " the
faith? Let us take two facets as examples:

a. The gospel is a demand for a " new life," a break with
   the past, a " dying to the old self."
b. Those who " die " to their old selves will be "raised " to
   newness of life by Christ.

The baptismal service enacts both. As the early Christian was submerged beneath the water, he " died." (If he were kept there, he really would.) He entered the tomb. And then, when he was raised up from the water, this dramatized the fact that a new life had now begun. The believer had been " raised " from the dead, he had emerged from the tomb. As Paul put it, he had died and risen with Christ. He had begun the life of " the new being in Christ Jesus." This is what is dramatized in the service of adult Baptism.

" But why babies? "

The above paragraphs are difficult enough. But why baptize babies, since they have no idea of what is going on, and probably take a dim view of the whole business?

We cannot claim that of two babies, the one who is not baptized goes to hell, while the one baptized has a free ticket to heaven. What the service " does " for the baby is to offer him openly, and in the sight of all, something that he already possesses — the love and grace of God, and the pledge of concern and care on the part of parents and congregation. The child is not aware of this, but *the deed has been done,* and later on he will have to accept it or reject it. Similarly a child, through no doing of his own, receives citizenship in his native country at birth. Later on he must decide whether to exercise it responsibly or not.

Infant Baptism dramatizes the gospel of God's grace — the fact that he seeks us out in love even before we seek him out, even before we are aware of his existence. God in Christ seeks out this child in love, even before the child is aware of God. This child is from the very beginning of his life the object of God's love and concern, one whom God has claimed for his own. Nothing can change this. The child may later accept the gift or reject it, but the gift has been offered.

Thus the child is a means by which God's grace is enacted for the people of God assembled to witness and participate in the ceremony. God can use a weak and defenseless baby as the outward and visible sign of his inward invisible grace. Worshipers are reminded that they are dependent upon God, as is this baby; that God has visited and redeemed them, as he does this child; and that they are called upon to offer up their lives to his service, as this child must someday do also. This is why a " home Baptism " misses the point. Baptism is an act of the Church, and by the Church, but also *for* the Church, a means whereby God's grace " comes home " afresh to the people of God. To have the service without the congregation is like having the minister preach a sermon without anyone to listen.

This has been a long, hard chapter. But it has been making only one point — that the Church exists where the Word is preached and the sacraments truly administered.

All the rest of the Church's life follows from this.

We now turn to look at other aspects of the life of the Church. Although they are in different chapters, they are dependent upon the life of the Church as it centers in Word and sacrament. The Church must be an " active " Church, taking a responsible place in the community, enlisting its members and its funds in the enterprise of missions, the ecumenical movement, the rehabilitation of the alcoholic, the redemption of the world of business, and all the rest. But the people of God can fulfill their calling in those provinces only as they have listened to the Word of God spoken to them, and knelt together to receive the Bread of Life offered on their behalf by Jesus Christ their Lord.

CHAPTER

7

THE PROPHETIC TASK OF THE CHURCH
. . . Or, the Church Says *No* and *Yes*

"Churches and individual Christians who seek to
'glorify God' *only* through hymns and prayers and 'living a good life' are sinning against their God." — *The
Standing Committee on Social Education and Action,
Presbyterian Church in the United States of America,
1955.*

> "There is little cheer
>   For the Church's prophets,
>   If they interfere
>   With the Church's profits."
> — *Saint Hereticus*

A number of years ago a book was published called *The
Church Against the World*. It seemed a strange title, but it
contained a real truth. For the Church does not exist to pat the
world on the back; it exists, in part at least, to do the opposite,
to call the world to a fresh start. The Church must say *no* to
the world as it is.

But the no must be in context. We saw in the last chapter
that the Church says yes to Jesus Christ. But since the Church

78

cannot " serve two masters " it can never give an unconditional yes to anything else, the State, an economic system or even the Church itself. For the Church to say no to the world, to stand " against the world," is not to repudiate the world, but to affirm it in the only way a Christian can, as something that stands " under God " and in need of redemption.

The perennial objection:

" Religion and politics don't mix."
> — *About 85 per cent of American laymen, and an*
> *unpleasantly large percentage of ministers.*

There is a curious resentment on the part of many church people about the Church's getting " mixed up " in the affairs of society, whether racial, political, economic, national, or international. Perhaps they fear that their own positions will be criticized by the gospel; perhaps they persist in making the false distinction between " sacred " and " secular," that the Reformers repudiated so vigorously, or perhaps they have *seen* the Church at work, inflaming sectarian hatreds on issues like birth control, beer, and bingo. Their objections are familiar:

The Church should stay out of politics.

Ministers should " preach the gospel " and not talk about social issues.

Religion is an individual affair; the Church should concentrate on saving souls.

Now any person of even modest intelligence can see that these attitudes boil down to something like this:

Religion is important for about one hour of one day each week. What happens during that hour has no relationship to the other hours of men's lives.

Not so good. Not the Christian faith, anyway.

Why the Church must be " involved":

" The theologian calls it the reassertion of the incarnation; the businessman calls it getting unwarrantedly mixed up in politics." — *Sir George MacLeod.*

" Jesus is Lord."
        — *The earliest Christian creed, which carried with it the clear implication, " Caesar is not Lord."*

There can be no such thing as " side line " Christianity. The Christian cannot stand at the edge looking on. He must be in the thick of the struggle, taking sides and involving himself. Why?

1. Christian faith is corporate, not individualistic. Its intent is to redeem men from isolation into community. It seeks a redeemed *society,* not a world in which men live their lives apart from one another.

2. Jesus reminded his hearers that love of God and love of neighbor are the same. One does not just " love God." One loves God by loving his neighbor, seeing him as a child of God, as one for whom Christ died. So the Christian can never devote so much time to prayer that he forgets about the sick, the undernourished, the victims of discrimination.

3. The Reformation called men back to *all* of life. It insisted that God's " call " to men involves living in the midst of the sinful fallen world — where governments function, where trade and commerce exist, where nation takes up sword against nation. It is in *that* situation that the Christian must live and act.

4. The affirmation that " Jesus is Lord," rather than Caesar,

might seem to relieve the Christian of present-world responsibility. But as the early Christians soon discovered, it did not mean that Caesar's realm was to be neglected, but that Caesar's realm was to be transformed and reclaimed, in the name of the one true God.

5. Christians acknowledge that they are " strangers and pilgrims on earth," " seeking a homeland," and that they look forward " to the city which has foundations, whose builder and maker is God " (Heb. 11:13, 14, 10). This does not make this life irrelevant, but merely indicates the terms in which this life must be judged, found wanting, and redeemed. If the Christian seems out of step with the world, it is because, as Thoreau said in a quite different connection, " he hears the beat of another drum." *Because* he hears the beat of another drum he must help others hear it, and learn to march to a nobler rhythm.

No " party line ":

Worried Christian legalist: " Can a Christian dance? "
Dr. Maltby (after reflecting): " Well, some can, and some can't."

" That's all very well," someone may respond. " The Christian should be involved. Sure. *But not the Church.*"

But to raise this objection is to miss the point of what it means to be a Christian. For a Christian is not just a Christian " before God," but before God *and his neighbor*. He is always a Christian in community. If the Christian must be involved, so must the Church. From this, no retreat.

But it does not follow that there is *a* way in which the Church must be involved. It does not mean that church members should form a political party to vote other church members into office. It does not mean that there is a clear-cut "Christian" stand on labor legislation, a tariff bill, the best way to defeat racial segregation, or whether dancing is "Christian." *But it does mean that the Church has a responsibility in these areas and a stake in them all*. The Church may have no right to say that Candidate A is the Church's choice, but it must place its best minds to bear on the issues at stake between Candidates A and B, and offer its members an analysis of those issues *in the light of Christian faith and ethics*. The notion that there is a connection between loving God and going to ward meetings may come as a shock. But it is important.

There are some issues on which the Church can be clear. Issues that deprive persons of their status as children of God are issues on which the Church should be able to express a corporate voice. Racial segregation is a good example of the Church having said "too little too late." It is to the shame of the churches that they are among the last groups in the nation to abolish segregation from their "fellowships." The recent wave of super-Americanism, with its pathological suspicion of everyone who is not a flag waver, hater of the UN, and decrier of Europe and Asia, can never be accepted by a Church that is faithful to the gospel. Elevating one nation above all other nations, and pouring down scorn on all who were not born in the U.S.A., is only a modern way of saying that Caesar is Lord.

How is it done?

How is the Church to "take a stand"? It must do so in many ways.

1. *Pronouncements* are often scoffed at by experts in Christian ethics. And there is a twofold difficulty with pronouncements: (*a*) they give people an excuse for thinking that it is enough to speak without acting, and (*b*) they furnish evidence

of ecclesiastical hypocrisy, since there is such a wide gap between what the Church says and what it practices. Pronouncements are, nevertheless, part of its task, since they do express the corporate mind of the Church and help individuals who feel strongly about certain issues to know that they are not alone, but have the support of the Church.

2. Much of what the Church does must be done *through its members*. Laymen are responsible for implementing their Christian concern for society in practical ways. The prophetic dimension of Christian faith should challenge them to work on school boards, help administer housing plans, run for public office, work in political parties, " needle " Congressmen, and so on. Here is where the apparently unspectacular work of the Christian conscience in society probably accomplishes most.

3. There are also *direct things* that churches can do. The congregation that " adopts " a church in a war-torn area does more for international relations than a dozen statements. The congregation that actively welcomes members of minority groups does more for race relations than a score of pronouncements. Involvement in the missionary activities of its denomination, in the World Council of Churches, demonstrates actively that the Church is more than just a national group, and that it is part of an all-inclusive society, which is a *fact* in the world today. " The Christian congregation itself," as the report of the World Council at Evanston reminds us, " should be a visible center of community."

Recognition of a danger:

" I had rather see coming toward me a whole regiment with drawn swords, than one lone Calvinist convinced that he is doing the will of God." — *A seventeenth-century writer.*

" The theocratic state,
Which Calvin helped inaugurate,
Was sometimes something less than that,
For Calvin was an autocrat."

— Saint Hereticus

The danger is this. Overzealous churchmen, in their enthusiasm for a project, can easily become convinced that what they want to do is identical with the will of God. It is bad enough to kill one's fellow men, but it is infinitely more perverse when it is done in the name of the gospel, as was done hundreds of times in the Inquisition, and a number of times by the Reformers. Those who assume that there is a " Christian " blueprint for society need to consider whether they are not simply projecting the " American dream " upon the universe and then demanding that God bless it. The fact that Christians are finite and sinful means that their attempts to live in society will reflect their finitude and perpetuate their sin. The greatness of the Reformed tradition is that men *are* empowered to do God's will fearlessly, since " God alone is Lord of the conscience." The danger is that some zealous Reformer will be too sure that God's will is identical with his will. The Christian Church, no less than the " lone Calvinist," must always keep asking itself whether it is really God's will that is being done.

The minister and the layman:

" The preacher must be soaked in the Bible." *— Daniel Jenkins, a Congregational minister.*

" All persons in the above age groups are required to register for national service except lunatics, the blind, and ministers of religion." *— Notice in Great Britain in 1939, as the nation prepared for war.*

" If the good *abbé* had talked a little about religion, I think he would have mentioned everything." — *Louis XVI, after a long sermon.*

The minister has gotten short shrift in this book. Part of this has been intentional. The book is for laymen, and " the priesthood of all believers " means that everybody is " clergy." Still, ministers exist. What is the layman to do about them?

The great temptation is to put the minister in a class by himself and expect him to uphold the " moral standards " of the community. This is a denial not only of the priesthood of *all* believers, but also of the Reformation doctrine of vocation. The phrase " full-time Christian service " when applied exclusively to ministers, religious education directors, and missionaries is an almost blasphemous misunderstanding of the Protestant heritage. The lawyer is engaged in full-time Christian service when he is a lawyer of integrity. So is the carpenter or the plumber or the college professor.

We must not, then, let the minister be less than a " full person," or placed in the same category with lunatics and the blind. But it would not be enough to settle for the conclusion that the minister is only a person with certain functions (running a church) just as another person has certain functions (running a bank or a ball team). For the minister *is* " set apart " by his Church, through the act of ordination, called to do certain things of a special sort. He is called to preach the Word of God — to bring his life under the discipline of Bible study, so he can faithfully convey what the Bible says to his people about the ordering of life. He is called to administer the sacraments — to offer to his people food and drink for their souls. He is called upon to hear their confessions, to assure them of God's forgiveness, to proclaim to them the demands which God places upon them.

And here arises the minister's temptation. For he may be idolized. His people do, after all, usually see him with his best foot forward, and they are likely to assume that he is a cut above them spiritually and morally. Not only does this tempt the minister to spiritual pride, but it perverts the meaning of the church. The church becomes " Dr. High's church." Guests are asked to " Come and hear Dr. High this morning." Forgotten is the fact that it is Christ's Church, and that worship is not hearing Dr. High, but praising God. It is no wonder that Dr. High is tempted to be clever rather than Christian, original rather than Biblical, and to preach " success Christianity " rather than " the true and lively Word."

This means that Protestants ought to take " apostolic succession " more seriously. This does not mean believing in a chain of successors from Jesus right down to the present bishop of Rome. It does mean that there is a succession, in which the minister should stand — a succession of fidelity to the apostolic faith. When he faithfully proclaims the Word of God, recalls to men what God did in Jesus Christ, keeps alive the faith to which the apostles witnessed, then he stands in the true apostolic succession.

In this sense the minister *must* be the conscience of his congregation. If they forget that religion and politics cannot be separated, he must remind them. If they insist on segregated churches, he must call them to task, reminding them that Christ died for all men, black as well as white.

The layman must do these things too. The priesthood of all believers must be clothed with overalls and put to work. For the layman to love his neighbor means not only being concerned about the soul in his neighbor's body, it also means being concerned with whether or not he has soles on his shoes.

8

THE REFORMATION MUST CONTINUE

" The Church must be forever building, for it is forever decaying within and attacked from without." — *T. S. Eliot, in " The Rock."*

" The time has come for judgment to begin with the household of God." — *I Peter 4:17.*

" The Reformation must continue." — *Schleiermacher, P. T. Forsyth, L. P. Jacks, Paul Tillich, and a host of others.*

But the Church cannot be content to live in its stained-glass house and throw stones through the picture windows of modern culture. It must also say no to itself and be even more critical of its own life than it is of the society around it. It is disheartening that the Church so infrequently says no to itself. But it can, and in this fact lies the hope of the Church. For the Church to say no to itself is simply its way of saying yes to Jesus Christ, and refusing to try to usurp his place.

This is the secret of the Reformation. In faithfulness to Christ, the Church said no to much of its own life — and was thereby redeemed. The tragedy would be for people to say to-day, "The Reformation has been finished." No, what happened in the sixteenth century — the reforming of the Church in faithfulness to the gospel — must happen in every century. The Reformation must continue. It is never finished. Here are some areas where it is needed.

1. The Church is always tempted to confuse itself with God:

"We think it an abomination to put our confidence or hope in any created thing, to worship anything else than Him." — *The Genevan Confession (1536) on faith in God.*

"I always like a dog so long as he isn't spelt backwards." — *Father Brown, in " The Oracle of the Dog."*

The Reformers lived to make clear that "only God is God," and that no one else can usurp his place. This is the point of the sovereignty of God — that he alone is God. This is the point of justification by faith — that he saves us and we do not save ourselves. This is the point of the authority of Scripture — that his Word is the final authority, not our words. This is the point of the priesthood of all believers — that he can use anyone in the fulfillment of his purposes, and not just those whom the Church designates for holy office.

But it is always a temptation to deny this fact. It is scarcely enough to point at the Roman Catholic doctrine of infallible authority, for Protestants have their own infallibilities. There are Protestants who would feel that they were somehow " attacking God " if they were to be critical of the Church, whereas if they were really concerned to be faithful to God, they might have to be particularly critical of the Church. There are Protestants who give their pastor's words quite as "infallible" a stamp as a Roman Catholic does to an ex cathedra statement. There are Protestants who claim such finality for the Church that they feel that anyone not formally identified with the Church is forever damned.

Can this latter claim, particularly, be maintained with quite the dogmatic finality of the Reformers? Granted that to be a Christian is to be within the Church, can we be sure who is "in" the Church and who is not? We have it on high authority that the prostitutes will enter the Kingdom of God ahead of some of the "righteous."

2. *The Church is always tempted to irrelevance:*

"[Calvinism is] a faith which is at its noblest when it is fighting and which after the battle has to guard against the danger of becoming muscle-bound." — *Erik Routley, who is a Calvinist.*

"A live heresy is better than a dead orthodoxy." — *P. T. Forsyth, who was not a heretic.*

The Church can become irrelevant by stressing the wrong things. Luther rediscovered the vitality of "faith" as trust in God. Within about a generation, the "Lutherans" (who also can become muscle-bound) had transformed faith into assenting to certain creeds and doctrines. The freshness gave way to a wooden orthodoxy.

Emil Brunner has shown how easy it is for the Church to do this. The Word is secured, he writes, and is replaced by creed and dogma. Fellowship is secured, and is replaced by institutions. Faith acting in love is secured, and is replaced by moral codes. In each case, a source of new vitality and life is stifled.

The Church becomes irrelevant by indifference. It becomes so intent to preserve its own way of doing things (forms, customs, ceremonies, certain vocabulary) that it fails to notice that its way of doing things is not reaching people. The antidote is not for the Church to junk its heritage and start from scratch with "the modern mind" (whatever that is), but rather to take the modern mind into account as it orders its life afresh from day to day in the light of the gospel.

This is not the place to enter into a discussion of the problem of "communication," which is a hornets' nest among contemporary church thinkers. It *is* the place to urge that laymen steal a page from the book of the modern skeptics, and keep asking their pastors and theologians: "What do you mean by that? What do you mean by that?" until between them they have hammered out an understanding of the Christian faith which is comprehensible and relevant. No layman needs to be told how irrelevant most preaching sounds, no matter how "orthodox" it may be. In this situation it is part of the layman's godly duty to raise a few agonizing howls.

What is needed is a fresh understanding of the relationship of freedom and tradition. Freedom, without tradition, goes berserk. Tradition, without freedom, becomes irrelevant. The solution is not to scrap one or the other, but keep both in tension. This involves seeing modern man and his needs *in the light of the gospel,* and it involves seeing the gospel, not in a vacuum, but in terms of *how it can speak compellingly to modern man.* The task is not easy but it is not impossible. There are few better treatises on what is meant by "original sin" than the headlines of a morning newspaper. Biblical insights about anxiety receive confirmation in psychoanalysis. There *are* resources. It is only when the Church refuses to gaze upon the world that it becomes irrelevant.

3. The Church is always tempted to perpetuate divisions:

> " ' We worship God in different ways,'
>   A layman says, intent to please.
> ' It matters not what forms we use,
>   So long as we are on our knees.' "

> " A haughty cleric makes reply
>   In unctuous words which go like this:
> ' You worship Him in your way,
>   I'll worship Him in His.' "
>
> *— Saint Hereticus*

Denominations are not necessarily the work of the devil. But when a denomination assumes that it alone has final Christian truth, then the cloven hoof is near, and the air is full of sulphur. There would be something ridiculous, if it were not so pathetic, about the way various branches of Christendom parade as the " true Church," and proceed to " unchurch " one another as " irregular " or as possessing " invalid ministries."

And as a result we have the shocking spectacle of Christians, who ought to be closest to each other at the common Table Christ provided for them, being at that one point unable to enter into full Communion with one another.

All this in the name of One who intercedes to God on behalf of his children, " that they may be one " (John 17:11).

4. The Church is always tempted to be fashioned by the world instead of refashioning the world:

> " The hippo's feeble steps may err
>   In compassing material ends,

While the True Church need never stir
To gather in its dividends."
       — *T. S. Eliot, comparing the Church*
       to " The Hippopotamus "

    Christianity Is Revolutionary.
       — *Book title by Maurice Fraigneaux*

It is unfortunately true that a church set in a " middle class " locale tends to reflect middle-class attitudes, while a church in an " industrial " area tends to reflect attitudes that prevail there. This is disturbing because it suggests that the Church has no discernible influence on the lives of its people, but that on the contrary it is " conditioned " by the attitudes people bring to it. It is easy to use the heroism of Christians in churches behind the iron curtain as an excuse for inaction on our part, but it needs to be remarked that the stern stuff of which certain Christians are made in East Berlin or Communist China is too little in evidence in American Protestantism.

It is true that the Church seldom stirs " to gather in its dividends," where it ought often to be casting a disturbed glance in the direction of those dividends. It is true that the Church seldom challenges the political convictions of its members. It is true that one can go to fashionable Protestant churches for years and never learn of anything at fault with America, the individual in the pew, or the fashionable Protestant churches. It is true that the " American Way of Life " is often held up as the precise equivalent of the " Christian way of life," so that church life simply mirrors American life and never challenges it.

The notion that the Christian community is to be a " minority " witness to the truth would sound strange to the average congregation. The notion that " Christianity is revolutionary " would strike many Protestant laymen as highly suspect, demanding Congressional investigation. Rather than transforming culture into something conformable to the will of God, the Church becomes content to be transformed into something conformable with American culture. In saying yes so unambiguously to its culture the Church says no to its Lord.

Are there signs of hope?

"It is the business of the Church to let the reality of a reconstituted community be visible in its own life, and to be constantly wary lest the reality of the new humanity be obscured by Church abuses, either of disunity, apostasy, or idolatry." — *Alexander Miller, in* The Renewal of Man.

It is not enough to ask, "Where is the reformation most needed?" We must also ask, "Are there any signs that reformation is in fact taking place?"

We shall not treat this question as exhaustively as the former. It is too easy to become self-satisfied and lose the zeal for ongoing reformation. As a reminder of this, we shall print this part of the chapter in smaller type. Where *is* fresh vitality to be found in the Church?

1. The first area will hardly strike the layman as exciting, and yet it is crucial. This is the *theological revival* which is going on in Protestantism.

The familiar plea of the layman, "Don't talk theology, talk common sense," is being shown up as a contradiction in terms. Any Christian who loves God "with all his mind" and starts to think through, or explain, his faith, is talking theologically. The option is never "theology" or "no theology." The option is always "good theology" or "bad theology." Thus the fact that there is theological ferment in modern Protestantism is a sign of vitality. It is a sign that Protestants are not stagnant, but are trying to rethink the meaning of their faith. And this can never be the exclusive duty of the professional theologians. It is a layman's task too — which is one reason why there must be laymen's " theological libraries." Nor should laymen be so afraid of the theologians. To read Reinhold Niebuhr's *Beyond Tragedy* or Paul Tillich's *The Shaking of the Foundations* should excite any literate Protestant.

2. The clearest expression of vitality within Protestantism is *the ecumenical movement*. From *oikumene* (" the inhabited world ") has come the word that describes a new reality in man's experience — that of Christians bound together across national, racial, and geographical barriers. The ecumenical movement (of which the World Council of Churches is the clearest embodiment) does not pretend to be a new " super church." But it does provide an arena where Churches can work together for the healing of the nations, and can confront each other in the midst of their ecclesiastical arrogance and concern, to learn from one another.

When the World Council, meeting in Amsterdam in 1948, said, " We intend to stay together," it marked a great moment in the history of Christendom. For it meant that the tendency of Protestants to split into more and more divisions was being replaced by the desire to unite. It is not necessarily to be desired that all denominations be welded into one, but the World Council offers a way through which Christendom can grow from strength to strength, ready to be used by God in whatever ways he may choose.

3. Another sign of vitality, an outgrowth of the ecumenical movement, is the fresh voice of the so-called " *younger churches,*" churches in countries where Christianity has only recently been a " live " religion, India, Japan, Korea, Thailand, and such. Here are Christians living where the " world revolution " is most intense, and where being a Christian involves hardship and risk. They have a resultant clarity of understanding and depth of commitment that are not only a witness to the world, but a challenge to Christendom. That Presbyterians, Methodists, Congregationalists, and Episcopalians in India have formed the United Church of South India,

shows that Christians *can* unite, and the achievement stands as a judgment on the churches of America and Europe.

The "world church" is a *fact,* a fact which cannot be discounted. Granted the fact is far from fullness, it is nevertheless a sign of vitality in the life of God's people.

4. The Reformation continues in *prophetic movements within the Church.* Here and there little groups rise up which, remaining within the Church, seek to call it back from studied mediocrity to prophetic witness.

There has been a movement within the Church of Scotland known as the Iona Community, a group of churchmen, both lay and cleric, who have been concerned that a dead Church come alive through a fresh discovery of the gospel. They insist that Christians must be involved politically, they busy themselves with slums and housing, they undertake an economic discipline; but they do all this under the discipline of the gospel, and in the context of Biblical faith and corporate worship.

An American example is the East Harlem Protestant Parish, in New York City. Here is a group ministry, men and women, lay and clerical, who are taking the Church to those in the slums, rather than waiting for those in the slums to make their way to the churches on the parksides. These people meet in "store front" churches; they help fight unscrupulous landlords; they lead crusades against police graft; they campaign for political office; they fight the "dope" racket — but they do it all in the name of Jesus Christ, who loves all men and in whom all men must be loved.

5. A final example of the continuing Reformation within the life of the Church is *the new emergence of the layman.* Protestantism has been too long under the "tyranny of the pastor," who often assumes that he runs the show and that the laymen are simply there to do his bidding.

But if the priesthood of all believers is *true,* then only as the layman is strong can Protestantism be strong. Laymen, individually and in groups, are beginning to wrestle with questions about the destiny of the Church. What does it mean to be an Evangelical Church? What is the layman's part in spreading the gospel? How does he " preach " the gospel in all that he does?

This particular sign of new vitality we shall not further describe. To do so might be to suggest that the job has been done, whereas the point is to remind that the job needs doing.

So it is not only appropriate, but necessary, to end this book on an indefinite note. A book about the Church can never be finished. Nor, particularly, can a chapter on the continuing Reformation. The last chapter in the life of the people of God can be written only by God himself.

And until that day, Christian folk must, in ways now known and ways no man knows yet, witness to God's mighty works and call all men into the inheritance he has in store for them, remembering the promise:

"You are a chosen race, a royal priesthood, a holy nation, God's own people, that you may declare the wonderful deeds of him who called you out of darkness into his marvelous light. Once you were no people but now you are God's people; once you had not received mercy but now you have received mercy." — *I Peter 2:9, 10.*